# HOW TO BURY A
# GOLDFISH

## ...and 113 other family rituals for everyday life

BY VIRGINIA E. LANG
AND
LOUISE B. NAYER

Daybreak Books
An Imprint of Rodale Books

© 2000 by Virginia E. Lang and Louise B. Nayer
Cover illustrations © by Jennifer Bolten
Interior illustration © by Sarah Patten

Cover Designer: Tanja Cole
Interior Designer: Joanna Williams
Cover Illustrator: Jennifer Bolten
Interior Illustrator: Sarah Patten

The poem "White Flowers" on pages 233–34 is reprinted by permission of Mary Oliver.

**Library of Congress Cataloging-in-Publication Data**

Lang, Virginia E.
    How to bury a goldfish : and 113 other family rituals for everyday life / by Virginia E. Lang and Louise B. Nayer.
       p.    cm.
    ISBN 1–57954–275–1 hardcover
    1. Family life—United States. 2. Family recreation—United States.
I. Nayer, Louise. II. Title.
HQ535.L34   2000
306.85—dc21                        00–029525

**Distributed to the book trade by St. Martin's Press**

2   4   6   8   10   9   7   5   3   1   hardcover

Visit us on the Web at www.rodalebooks.com, or call us toll-free at (800) 848-4735.

OUR PURPOSE

*We publish books that empower people's minds and spirits.*

DAYBREAK

*Dedicated to my Aunt Margaret, whose unwavering belief in my worth has been a constant inspiration and support; to my husband, Dean, whose love and encouragement sustains me in my work and my vision; to my stepdaughter, Heather, for her insight and support; to my daughter, YuWen, who is the light of my life and a constant reminder of what is good and true; and to my mother, who always wished she had the words for things*

—V. Lang

*Dedicated to my loving family and friends, young and old, for your belief in my writing; and for my husband, Jim, whose unselfish love guides me and frees me; and for Sarah and Laura, daughters of my soul and pure joy*

—L. Nayer

# Contents

## Beginnings 🐟

## Fabulous Firsts 🐟

## Red-Letter Days 🐟

## Transitions 🐟

## Loss

## Holidays

# Acknowledgments

For their encouragement and support, I wish to thank Margaret Bauer; Mary Rowse; George Lang; the late Frederick Lang; Heather Michelson; Ellen and Mark Borenstein; Peter and Nick Borenstein; Emily Defraites; Sharon Swinyard; David Sutton; Ray Ling Hou Chang; Ken Petron; Panna Flower; Diana Condon; Nitza Agam; Mitani D'Antien; Americo Yabar; Susan Eisenberg; Gail Grimes; Claude Whitmyer; Rosario Fernandez; Ann Mayer Heselwood; Carole Garland; Jim Eilers; Judy Maselli; Sarah Patten; Laura Patten; Morgan Green; Louise Bennett; Rita Rine; Aldona Watts; Myrna Chapman; Barbara Le Maire; Alexis Arrow; Peggy Luke; Judy McCarthy; Bill Pinder; the Kimmel, Maruzka, Wellington, Federico, Martin, and Green families; and the staff of the Countryside Market of Swarthmore, Pennsylvania. Special thanks to Sheree Bykofsky, our agent, and to Christian Millman, whose patience, intelligence, and kindness helped the process match the message.

—V. Lang

For their love and guidance, I first want to thank my parents, Dorothy and Hank Nayer; also Anne Nayer and Lily McMenamin; Bonnie Patten and George Brencher; Janice Bressler; Josee Andrei; Bill Wallace; Jeri McGovern; the people at the Unitarian Church, including Pat Post, John Marsh, Barbara Conahan, and Betsy Darr; Jim Eilers; Myrna Chapman; Barbara Le Maire; Aldona Watts; Alexis Arrow; Peggy Luke; Claire Thurston; Mimi Fried; Leslie Simon; Anita and Elizabeth Strong; Dr. Rong Rong Zheng; YuWen Michelson Lang; Laura Patten, Sarah Patten, and Jim Patten; Lynn Levy; Cathy DeRosas and Penny Speckter; Nina Lathrop; and in memory of Reverend and Mrs. Daubert.

Special thanks to Sheree Bykofsky for believing in the book and to Christian Millman, our editor, a man of intelligence, kindness, and grace.

—L. Nayer

# Introduction

The sun rises, an enormous ball of fire thousands of miles wide, yet we hardly notice. Alarm clocks buzz unmercifully in our dark rooms and, as if on automatic pilot, we do our morning duties, alone or with family, only subliminally aware of the magic that has just occurred. The sun has risen once again and the darkness has vanished, but we have not been a part of it.

How do we see the magic in each day and connect with the natural world, our fellow humans, ourselves?

In a time when many people are struggling simply to survive, we are constantly bombarded with hollow materialism; stores open 7 days a week, beckoning us; and demands of work and family far exceeding our ability to respond. In our hearts, we know that something is missing, that we are not fully present in our own lives, that the carousel of busyness and consumerism is spinning faster and faster, placing in jeopardy the very Earth on which we live. We have traded lighted candles and soft shadows for the neon glare of computer screens and the bleeps and blips of our technological toys.

How, then, do we reclaim the very part of us that makes us human? How do we establish a loving pace amid the rush and chaos?

This book is a guide to noting and celebrating the everyday events of our lives: marking the passage of a young girl into womanhood; helping a single friend begin a new home life; taking time to fully mourn the death of a loved one; feeling that it is okay, even right, to turn on the answering machine and simply sit in silence. The nights we light a candle for a loved one who is ill or help a young child celebrate a difficult school decision are nights we cherish and remember, times when we slow down and fill our lives with softness and caring for each other.

We, the authors, met 13 years ago at the Blue Danube Cafe on Clement Street in San Francisco. Our meeting was co-incidental—one woman, Ginny, talking to another woman, Louise, who was breastfeeding her daughter Sarah and welcomed Ginny's openness. We found out we knew people in common from the East Coast and realized, as we got together more and more often, how much we had in common and how much we both wanted to build a community embracing family and friends, young and old, and especially children in our circle of love.

Along with our shared vision, we came to write this book inspired by our individual journeys. For Louise, this book is threaded with the voices of her grandfather Joseph Daubert, a Presbyterian minister in upstate New York, and her great-great-grandfather Lazarus Nayer, a rabbinical scholar on the Lower East Side. Her ancestry is grounded in the life of the spirit. More important, as a poet for many years, Louise has been inspired by both women and men, their struggles, their language, and their courage to speak the truth. Over the past years, Louise and her family have attended the Unitarian Church, a church that embraces all religions and all people. Some of the traditions in the book were inspired by Unitarian practices.

Ginny was influenced by her aunt and godmother, Margaret Bauer, for many years a teacher of young children in Philadelphia, now 95 years of age. Aunt Margaret's tremendous warmth and personal faith have given Ginny a portrait of true grace and inner strength. Beyond family influences — she was raised in a German Lutheran family — Ginny's journey toward adoptive motherhood and subsequent trip to China, as well as her work and travel with Peruvian shaman Amerigo Yabar, have influenced her understanding of the mystical nature of the world and of her place in it. Ginny shares Louise's love of poetry and words and began writing in a poetry workshop led by Louise, which evolved into a writing group that still meets many years later. Ginny is the godmother of Louise's girls, Sarah and Laura.

After years of cherished memories — sharing birthdays, job challenges, the deaths of parents, and the many small victories in the lives of children — we decided it was time to write down some of the ceremonies and rituals that had meaning for us, in the hope that others could benefit.

We are not looking to replace ancient truths or the community and faith that can be found in a place of worship, but we have found useful and heartfelt ways to express ritual and ceremony in lives that embrace blended families and differing cultural backgrounds and lifestyles. In addition, we have written and discovered some beautiful words to give voice to the feelings we all experience at poignant times in our lives.

The book's title was inspired by an event common in

many households with young children, the death of a pet gold-fish. Both of us have befriended and buried small animals, grieved for the loss of elders, celebrated friends' decisions to change careers, and honored the many milestones in children's lives. As with the fish burial, we offer ideas for simple cere-monies—some based on time-honored practices, others com-pletely new—that can be done in a short time and can be easily adapted to any reader's lifestyle.

We have written a "family" book because we believe that we all have family, however we choose to define it. Traditions for singles are included, such as a "shower" for a young man get-ting his first apartment and an annual celebration for a single person who is special in the life of a family.

We believe our everyday lives deserve celebration. As our world grows more complex, it takes more thought to do less. Through simple ritual and ceremony, we slow down and open our eyes to the beauty and meaning in our lives, awakening to the natural world and the richness of our relationships with others. When we take time to see the sun rise and set, to really see the exploding colors of the universe, we awaken ourselves from cynicism and despair and open our hearts to the mysteries of nature, our bodies, our lives.

This book is an offering. We hope you will accept it as an invitation to take time and to fully experience what is most im-portant in life: family, friends, and the many wonders of our everyday lives.

# EVERYDAY RITUALS

*It is in the everyday events of our lives that we express who we are. When we rush through our day focused only on our destination, we are not fully alive, not able to see and savor the precious moments that fill our daily lives: letting water cleanse us in the morning, acknowledging coworkers instead of hurriedly racing past to our offices, sitting quietly around a dinner table at twilight, and lighting a candle before each meal. Every day offers us rich opportunities for renewal.*

# Waking: Greeting the Day in Peace

*Earth, ourselves,*
*breathe and awaken,*
*leaves are stirring,*
*all things moving,*
*new day coming,*
*life renewing.*
*—Pawnee prayer*

Getting up and out in the morning is often a purple haze of activity—gulps of coffee, toast on the run, and hastily blown kisses while scrambling to find the bookbag, the keys, the homework, and the briefcase. It seems the day has legs and is already running away before it even begins. It takes determination and ritual to take back the morning. Even if you hate mornings and can't function until your second cup of coffee, easing into morning may help you center yourself and reclaim your day.

## 🐟 WHAT YOU NEED 🐟

- *A Zen chime available at many department stores; or a clock radio;*
- *An uplifting photo of someone you love or a special painting*

## 🐟 WHAT YOU DO 🐟

*There are many gentle alarm clocks now available; some offer sounds of nature, others vibrate you awake! Try waking* to the quiet and calm of a Zen chime that slowly pings in intervals that gradually shorten. Or simply get a clock radio and set it to a classical or soothing station. Once awake, turn it off and let your eyes rest on a photo or painting you love that is hung in your direct line of vision. Then, take a simple body inventory while still in bed. Notice the sensation in your ankles, your legs, and so on until you have slowly climbed up your body to your head.

Then, take a minute to reflect on your current situation, the demands of the day, picturing yourself moving smoothly and easily from task to task.

Finally, think about the people you most love and focus on their whereabouts and well-being this day. Picture your safe return home after a satisfying day.

# Calling Your Body from Sleep

*May my body*
*Be a prayerstick*
*For the world.*
*—Joan Halifax*

The first moments of our day set the tone for the rest of it. When we leap out of bed to the sound of an alarm clock, rush to shower and dress and gulp down a quick breakfast, we are not fully present in our day. We are abusing our bodies instead of honoring them in a spirit of gratitude. Our bodies support us in everything we do, yet we often ignore them and take them for granted.

Theologian Matthew Fox speaks of awakening our spiritual and physical energy through chakra work. The chakras are important intersections in the body where energy is especially concentrated. There are seven master chakras in the body, each with its own distinct function. The ritual that follows is an attempt to make contact with each of these powerful junctions in our bodies and to evoke, in a conscious way, their full potential. In Eastern thought, this is inviting "the uncoiled serpent that lies sleeping at the base of our spine to gloriously unwind."

## ✦ WHAT YOU NEED ✦

- *Five minutes in bed, lying quietly*
- *A Meditation for the Chakras*

# ☙ WHAT YOU DO ❧

Begin each day by placing both hands at the appropriate chakra and inviting yourself to be present in the day with these words.

## A Meditation for the Chakras

BASE OF YOUR SPINE
*"May I be grounded in the deepest pulse of the Earth, connected to the source of all life."*

LOWER ABDOMEN (just below your navel)
*"May I live with passion and commitment this day."*

SOLAR PLEXUS (just below your heart)
*"May I be powerful, bringing purpose and direction to all I do."*

HEART
*"May my heart expand with compassion toward others."*

THROAT
*"May I speak my truth."*

FOREHEAD
*"May I bring my fullest knowing and creativity to life."*

TOP OF YOUR HEAD
*"May I praise the good work of others."*

When you have finished, put your feet on the ground and take three deep breaths, picturing yourself moving easily and gracefully, bringing your best to your day.

# Morning Shower:
# A Daily Renewal

*Dewdrop, let me cleanse*
*in your brief*
*sweet waters . . .*
*These dark hands of life*
*—Basho*

Water is used in many rituals throughout the world. It is a symbol of purity and cleansing; in baptism, it signifies new life and renewal. We have the opportunity to embrace this feeling of renewal every time we step into the shower or bath, if we take just a minute to let in the wonder of water.

## 🐟 WHAT YOU NEED 🐟

- A shower or bathtub
- A natural sponge

## 🐟 WHAT YOU DO 🐟

As you shower, luxuriate in the incredible gift of water. Our bodies are mostly water; our planet is covered in water; water and sunshine make it possible for plants to thrive. Take your sponge and let the water fill it to saturation. Then, squeeze it over your head, letting the water run down your face and arms—take in its warmth, its refreshment, its silky sensation as the water purifies all troubles from the previous day and night.

Repeat this until you are ready to em
completely fresh and renewed.

Hang a copy of this beautiful pass
ture near your shower and read it as yo

O Waters, give us health, bestow on us
Vigor and strength, so shall I see enjoyn
Rain down your dewy treasures o'er our
Like loving mothers, pour on us your blessing,
Make us partakers of your sacred essence.
We come to you for cleansing from all guilt,
Cause us to be productive, make us prosper.
—Rig-Veda

# The Family Sandwich:
# A Tasty Morning
# Send-off

*The only emperor is the emperor of ice cream.*
*—Wallace Stevens*

YuWen's father is a very big man. One of the things he likes to do first thing in the morning is to smother YuWen and me in his big arms in a "family sandwich." At first I'd be the pastrami, he'd be the cheese, and YuWen would be the pickle. Then, each new day, we'd all pick new identities. Over time, we have evolved into a sundae (more appealing to a 4-year-old) and we change flavors and toppings each day.

I believe funny little rituals take on the importance this one has for us because, in this small gesture each day, we demonstrate to YuWen that we are a family and that she is an equal player in this family. I know that as a petite only child living with two much older, much bigger people, she must find it hard to remember that she has a distinct place and is a key "ingredient." It's also just a lot of fun to do!   —V. Lang

## WHAT YOU NEED

- *About 1 minute before leaving the house*
- *A place to gather*

## 🐟 WHAT YOU DO 🐟

Just before leaving the house in the morning, say, "Time for the family sandwich." Have each person pick an ingredient that suits him that day. Some days are pastrami, some are cold turkey. Let each person pick what he wants, no matter how crazy the sandwich gets; we've had marshmallows-with-liverwurst days! Then, squeeze the sandwich together in a huge hug and have everybody take a bite (kiss) of each other's parts.

# A Workplace Ritual: Checking In with Your Heart

*I wish I loved the human race;*
*I wish I loved its silly face;*
*I wish I liked the way it walks;*
*I wish I liked the way it talks;*
*And when I'm introduced to one*
*I wish I thought,* What jolly fun!
—*Sir Walter Raleigh*

I am not a morning person. When someone tries to talk to me before I've had my coffee, they are met with a half-hearted groan. My husband, on the other hand, is painfully cheerful the minute his eyes open. After 14 years, he still talks to me in the morning as if I were *there.*

When I worked in a hospital, many meetings were held early to accommodate physicians' schedules. I hated these sessions and missed most of what was said.

Whether you work in an office, a school, or a bakery, you start the day or night with human beings, in all their quirks and splendors. Some have come to work charged up with ideas and enthusiasm; others have come in angry from some household grumble; still others are just not awake! If the day is to be productive and pleasant, we need to recognize each other's individuality and offer a measure of compassion to those who may be troubled in some way.   —V. Lang

## 🐟 WHAT YOU NEED 🐟

- Ten minutes
- A place to meet as a group

## 🐟 WHAT YOU DO 🐟

Ask your work group to sit around a table, preferably in a circle, for a 10 minute check-in. Have each person take 1 to 2 minutes to acknowledge the group and to convey any big news in his life. It may be a personal anecdote such as "My cat ran away last night and my children are very upset," or a simple expression of gratitude to be back with the group after a vacation or illness. If you have a rambler in your group, you may need to appoint one person each morning to call time at the 2-minute maximum. Gently remind the group of Shakespeare's adage "Brevity is the soul of wit."

After each person speaks, the group should say together, "May we offer our best to each other this day." Though it takes just a few minutes, this practice invites each person to be present, to feel heard, and to remember he is important in the lives of his coworkers.

# Writing as Ritual Time

*Take a pen in your uncertain fingers.*
*Trust, and be assured*
*That the whole world is a sky-blue butterfly*
*And words are the nets to capture it.*
—Muhammad al-Ghuzzi (Tunisian poet)

Everyone is a writer. Whether you write for a living or for pleasure, every one of us can benefit from taking the time to put thoughts and feelings on paper. I have written many exhaustive imaginary letters that helped me to clarify a feeling or resolve a relationship. Though they were seldom sent, they helped me to move forward and, later, to remember what I was feeling at a particular time.

Julia Cameron, in her beautiful book *The Artist's Way*, suggests starting each day with three "morning pages," just to get engaged. I take this idea one step further and say to myself, *Just write three* bad *pages*, so I will lighten up and not take myself so seriously. Give yourself the permission to be uninspired and to simply write. You may find the simple joy of self-expression is a useful way to begin each day, no matter where it leads.   —V. Lang

## ☙ WHAT YOU NEED ❧

- *A half-hour each morning*
- *Good tea or coffee in a mug only for you*
- *A journal*
- *A pen*

- ... *Perchance to Dream: A Lullaby Album for Children and Adults* by Carol Rosenberger

## ➤ WHAT YOU DO ➤

If you go to an office each day, arrive a half-hour before your work is to begin. If you are at home, get the kids off, eat breakfast, get dressed, turn on the answering machine, and go to the quietest place in your home with your tea or coffee. Take out your journal and pen, sit down, and begin to write. If you have trouble getting started, you may find it helpful to write to someone—a friend, a boss, someone not living—someone you admire or are angry with. Play ... *Perchance to Dream* or another soothing recording.

Write three journal pages without lifting your pen from your paper. Avoid judgment and do not edit what you write. If you want to rewrite something you are proud of and want to develop further, do so at another time. This practice is for self-expression only. Over the months, this can become a wonderful ritual of deep connection and self-care.

# Meditation for a Child

*Then river waves are calmed.*
*—Li Ch'i*

My daughter Laura once said that adults often don't realize that children have a lot of stress. For starters, schools give a lot more homework than they did years ago. Competitive sports, which used to start in high school, now begin at the early age of 6 or 7. Today, many children have less time to dream, for a myriad of reasons: they are overscheduled, both parents are working, or the streets don't feel safe, and parents respond by finding programs to keep their children occupied.

Even though my schedule allowed me to pick up Laura after school every day, and she could come home and rest, she still felt stress from school and soccer.

At age 11, she started developing exercise-induced asthma after joining a traveling soccer team. We decided to see a Chinese doctor, Dr. Rong Rong Zheng, recommended to us for her expertise in treating asthma. What helped Laura the most, I believe, in her treatment was the meditation she learned.

After going to Dr. Zheng, Laura said, "Soon, I had learned how to meditate. This relaxation cleared my mind. My brain was finally breathing, finally resting." The meditation helped Laura immeasurably with her asthma and her homework. Dr. Zheng said that children who do her "medical meditation" complete their homework in much less time and retain more. Most important, they are relaxed and their bodies are better able to deal with stress.   —L. Nayer

## WHAT YOU NEED

- Time alone, twice a day—once in the morning and once in the afternoon or evening before doing homework

## WHAT YOU DO

Go into a quiet room and close the door. Do not turn on any music or the TV. Sit cross-legged and, if you can, put your ankles on the opposite knees, yoga style.

Lace your fingers together with your thumbs touching, creating a circle of energy throughout your body. Put your hands at the bottom of your stomach, near your belly button.

Breathe deeply, using your stomach rather than your chest. Say the number 1 in your mind. Continue until you reach the number 50 (or beyond) if you wish. Feel the oxygen flowing through your body; think of nothing else but your breathing.

When you are finished, sit with your hands still laced together and your thumbs touching. Rub your clasped hands in a circle against your body, up to the top of your chest and down, starting from your belly button. Do that 10 times, breathing deeply as you do it.

# The Word Hat: Attracting Good Things

*Words are, of course, the most powerful drug*
*used by mankind. —Rudyard Kipling*

Leaving our homes is an important transition, but one we seldom notice. We leave behind the safe and secure dwellings that house our special people and special belongings for a world that brings chaos and challenge along with opportunity. Much of what happens to us is a result of how we prepare to meet the world and what we see in the thousands of stimuli we encounter in an average day. Words can be a powerful reminder that we attract what we think about.

## ✎ WHAT YOU NEED ✎

- *Index cards on which you have written words expressing qualities such as hope, perseverance, generosity, grace, forgiveness, clarity, and so on*
- *A hat with a flat bottom*

## ✎ WHAT YOU DO ✎

*Place the index cards in a hat. Keep the "word hat" by the front door. One day a week, let each person select one word from the hat to take along for the day. Later, at dinner, have each person share the word he got and how it "showed up" during the day. For example, a child who got the word for-*

*giveness* may see that she is holding a grudge against a friend that is festering with each day that they do not speak to each other. *Generosity* may inspire a new thought about a homeless person asking for money.

If there is no shared meal or natural opportunity to share thoughts, each person may choose to write a paragraph about his word in a journal.

# Cooking with Children

*Long before institutionalized religion came along with
temples and churches, there was an unquestioned
recognition that what goes on in the kitchen is "holy."*
—The New Laurel's Kitchen

Fermenting dough, churning butter to cream, caramelizing sugar—these are examples of kitchen alchemy, transformations that remind us of a larger hand at work. When I am cooking with YuWen, watching her little hands discover all the properties of flour or joyfully covering her mouth in chocolate, I am reminded that cooking with children is one of the most satisfying rites of our daily lives. Being with her and all the beautiful shapes, tastes, and textures of the living things we eat to nurture ourselves takes me to a magical place where time recedes and sensuality triumphs.   —V. Lang

## 🐟 WHAT YOU NEED 🐟

- *Time to cook*
- *Lots of fresh seasonal ingredients*
- *Willing children*

## 🐟 WHAT YOU DO 🐟

*One night a month, plan a family cooking night when the
meal will be prepared by the entire family. Select a menu with
fresh seasonal fruits and vegetables. Think about easy jobs to
match the age and experience level of each of your children. Be*

sure to invite and include elders to prepare and share this meal. Ask the children to set and decorate the table with festive, seasonal colors.

Guide your children to use their hands, simple tools, and their instincts when cooking. Notice and talk about the sounds of chopping, stirring, peeling; look at the rich textures and colors; savor the smells.

Some foods just lend themselves well to this type of hands-on event. Among them are corn on the cob, skewered summer vegetables, salads, fruit mixes, and baked goods. Let your imagination roam.

# First Fruits:
# A Seasonal Tradition

*To everything there is a season, and a time to every
purpose under the heaven. —Ecclesiastes 3:1*

Once, I had a Swiss cooking teacher who said, "If you have to ask
me for the recipe, you don't understand. A real cook goes to the
market, sees what is fresh and delightful, and celebrates the sensuality of each trip."

In our world of tasteless winter tomatoes, anemic strawberries, and limp, lifeless lettuce, markets (or, rather, *supermar-
kets*) are hardly sensual wonderlands. They are more like
packaging museums dedicated to carefully concealing each item's
flavor and texture behind layers of colorful plastic and cardboard.

Yes, we can now get peaches in winter and asparagus in
July, but we have lost the sense of the special, the thrill of seeing
blood-red strawberries come to market in June, full of flavor;
summer tomatoes that smell like the earth itself; corn so sweet
it bursts in your mouth. We want all of it, all of the time, so
nothing is special any of the time.

With this in mind, it seems especially fitting to mark the
end of a season or the beginning of a new one as especially precious, a moment to savor and celebrate.   —V. Lang

## ❧ WHAT YOU NEED ❧

- *A harvest calendar for your area (call a local fruit
  farmer for a reference or ask your state's Department*

of Food and Agriculture for a "Farmer to Consumer Directory")
- A family calendar
- A free weekend
- A good, complete fruit-and-vegetable cookbook, such as *The Joy of Cooking*

## 🐟 WHAT YOU DO 🐟

Make it a family ritual to celebrate the "first fruits" of each season. Refer to the harvest calendar to mark on your family's master calendar the weekends when each harvest will be in. Get directions to the farm nearest you that allows you to pick your own.

Invite another family to go along to the farm, and organize a two-family "cook in" to can tomatoes, bake peach pies, make delicious jellies and jams—whatever the season offers. Use the guidelines in an excellent cookbook on fruit and vegetable dishes. Rodale, the publisher of this book and long a leader in organic gardening and living, has many! Plan a celebratory dinner to enjoy the food; and at the meal, join hands and say, "Thank you for the bounty of the Earth and the abundance of this season."

If you don't like cooking, invite a favorite child or friend to go with you to gather the brilliantly fresh fruit as a seasonal ritual in itself. Be sure to pick too much and share it. Grandmothers who remember "fresh" will be especially pleased with a gift of raspberries or summer tomatoes and can often show you how to handle what you picked.

Here is an example of a harvest calendar, this one for the San Francisco Bay Area, from *Seasonal Expectations* by Katherine Grace Endicott.

- *Almonds—September and October*
- *Apples—July through October*
- *Apricots—June*
- *Berries—June and July*
- *Cherries—May*
- *Corn—July through August*
- *Figs—September through November*
- *Melons—June through October*
- *Oranges—December through February*
- *Peaches—July and August*
- *Pears—July through October*
- *Plums—July and August*
- *Pumpkins—October*
- *Tomatoes—August through October*
- *Walnuts—October through December*

# Tuning In to Twilight

*Opal mist descends*
*rounding jagged mountain peaks,*
*twilight is falling.*
—*Virginia Lang*

In every culture and time, contemplative silence has ritual importance. In the Jewish tradition, the family sits shivah when a loved one dies, honoring the deceased through shared silence. In Eastern religions, meditation is practiced as a way of going inside to a place of quiet and inner knowing.

In the Andes, the Q'ero Indians have a practice of sitting in meditative silence at twilight time, which they call the hour of power. They believe twilight is a particularly powerful time for gaining insights from within, reawakening us to our life's purpose. Observing the subtle change of light as the sun sets is a lesson in seeing, in breathing, and in being. It is nature's nightly light-and-sound show, free of admission, playing to audiences all over the world every single day of our lives.

## ☞ WHAT YOU NEED ☜

- A quiet place to sit outdoors
- A pillow and a blanket

## ☞ WHAT YOU DO ☜

Find a comfortable place to sit outside that is facing west. Take a pillow and blanket with you. Sit comfortably and just watch the colors as the sun slowly sets, naming them in your mind with descriptive words like *crimson, papaya, violet,* and *russet.* Be as creative as possible, really noticing the dimensions of color and naming each subtle shade.

Spend at least 10 minutes in total silence, watching the colors of day meld into the inky blue of night. Breathe deeply and let the concerns of the day fall away. Picture yourself taking off the tensions of the day as if you were undressing each concern one by one until you are lighter and freer. Stay as quiet and still as you can until you are covered in darkness.

# The Family Dinner

*"It's broccoli, dear."*
*"I say it's spinach, and I say the hell with it."*
—E. B. White

Evening is an excellent time to draw the family together and reflect on the experiences each person has had throughout the day.
Unfortunately, in many households, it is a time of gobbled food,
ringing phones, and the white noise of television in the back-
ground.

So, first decide to make the evening meal an occasion—
that is, begin with the understanding that when everyone is
seated no disturbances will be allowed to intrude. If the ringing
of an unanswered phone bothers you, turn the ringer off. If you
are accustomed to watching the news, tape it and watch it later
in the evening.

## ☙ WHAT YOU NEED ❧

- *A centerpiece candle of any size*
- *Willing hands*
- *Matches*
- *Selected readings*

## ☙ WHAT YOU DO ❧

Buy or make a special family candle just for the table.
Ask a family member to light the candle every night at the
start of the meal. Join hands and start to squeeze, passing the

squeeze from the first squeezer to the person on her right until it comes full circle to the person who started it. You may want to start with the youngest or eldest member present or with the one whose birthday is nearest. Then, raise the circle of hands and say, "Blessings on the meal!"

Ask, "Is there someone who needs special thoughts tonight?" Then, with hands still joined, send some silent thoughts of support to a person who may be ill or troubled in some way.

One night a week, choose a reader to read a short passage he has written or taken from a favorite book, as a way to introduce humor, literature, and beautiful words to your family table. Here is a short quip from Mark Twain to get you started: "Cauliflower is nothing but cabbage with a college education."

# Setting a Place for Elijah

*In spite of everything, I still believe that people are really good at heart.* —Anne Frank (1929–1945)

Many religions and cultures celebrate the sharing of meals. In the Jewish tradition of setting a place for Elijah, Elijah is the unseen guest who is always welcome at the family table. He is a reminder that no matter how little we may have, we always have something to share.

## WHAT YOU NEED

- A designated night of the week
- An extra place setting

## WHAT YOU DO

Choose a night of the week to set an extra place at the table. Ask a different member of the family to set the extra place each week. Since Elijah is a guest, his place may be a bit special.

When everyone is seated at the table, join hands and say together, "We welcome Elijah to our table. May we always remember there is enough to share."

Once a month, you may wish to invite someone new to your family to share a meal, in Elijah's place.

# Nighttime Prayer

*I wish the rain would help the flowers grow.*
*I wish a rose for my family.*
*I wish people would be happy forever.*
—*Laura Patten*

When she was small, my daughter Laura wrote this prayer during a bad drought season; hence, the wish for rain! For many nights over the years, she would say this prayer before bed. In its simple way, the prayer said all she wanted to about the Earth, her family, and the world.

The Unitarian Universalist (UU) Church encourages children to make up their own prayers. One particular bedtime ritual in the book that the Church gave Laura when she turned 8 helped her at nighttime to move into a place of beauty and rest. —L. Nayer

## ◆ WHAT YOU NEED ◆

- *A made-up prayer*
- *Bedtime prayer thoughts*

## ◆ WHAT YOU DO ◆

Help your child to make up her own prayer by first looking at these bedtime prayer thoughts. Then, have her recite her prayer each night. After the prayer, she can recite the bedtime prayer thoughts. Talk with her about each prayer thought, or think in silence together.

## Bedtime Prayer Thoughts for UU Kids

*Think about things you are THANKFUL for today*

*Think of something you feel SORRY that you said or did,*
*and any way you can make it right.*

*Think about something you HOPE will happen, and any*
*way you can help it to happen.*

*Think about being in a PLACE of BEAUTY or a FAVORITE*
*place where you feel safe and good.*

*Think about the people you love*
*and their love for you.*

*See each person's face in your mind.*

*Give them a goodnight smile!*

　　*—from the* UU Kids Book *by Charlene Brotman, Barbara Marshfield,*
　　*and Ann Fields*

# The Storytelling Stool

*Every day you see a dandelion floating in the sky as
big as a storm. —YuWen*

I love to tell stories. YuWen and I have a bedtime ritual that I also
enjoyed with my stepdaughter, Heather. The girls choose a character (either a person or an animal), the name of the character,
and where she lives. I take it from there and spin out a tale as
fantastic as I like until I hear the heavy breathing of slumber.
This has been extremely satisfying for me and very practical as a
sleep aid because it allows the story to be told in the dark!
When Heather was little, I had a special storytelling stool. Once
I sat on it, she settled down and got comfortable for the night.

Reading books out loud is also a wonderful nightly ritual
that many families observe. But I have found that live storytelling is especially intimate and creative (no one else has ever
heard this story before) and the girls really use their minds
trying to give me impossible combinations—like the green ele-
phant named Delicious that lives on Mars. I also learn what's up
in their magical minds, whether it's long-necked dinosaurs or
purple unicorns. Some nights on the stool have inspired some
really magical stories. YuWen's floating-dandelion mind really
responds to magic; the more bizarre, the better.   —V. Lang

## ❧ WHAT YOU NEED ❧

- *Time to tell a good long story*
- *A storytelling stool*
- *A character, a name, and a place*

## ➤ *WHAT YOU DO* ◄

Take your place on the storytelling stoo[l]
to start you off by answering the questions [W]
acter? What is her name? Where does she li[v]

Place no restrictions; just work with wha[t you get,] however challenging. Follow the basics of good storytelling: Present a conflict or dilemma for the character, then a moment of
crisis, then a resolution. For example, a blue unicorn from Mars
lands on Earth, can eat only daisies, is near starvation, but is
helped by grasshoppers to find a whole field of flowers!

You will get better with time and may come to find this
the most creative part of your day. Just be sure something happens in your story. Little children like an exciting plot, particularly one with a moral dilemma like unfairness or injustice, so
pose a dilemma for the character and solve it by the end.

You may wish to hand paint or stencil your storytelling
stool with the names of some of your memorable characters,
adding to it over time. It will be a wonderful souvenir of precious nights together.

# Healing Yourself: A Nightly Hug

*Stand still in this stone blade in the red cedar moon,*
*Listen to the shamans roam through stars.*
*—Duane Niatum*

When I was 4 years old and my sister, Anne, was 6, our parents were critically burned in a gas explosion. It happened while they were lighting a pilot light in the basement of a rented home in Cape Cod, Massachusetts. Anne and I were sleeping upstairs when the accident occurred.

At 42, the age at which my mother was burned and my own daughters were 4 and 6, I experienced panic attacks. In an effort to "get a hold of myself," I went to renowned hypnotist Isabel Gilbert, who has used hypnosis with people all over the world. She made a personalized tape for me that I still listen to and treasure.

Toward the end of the tape, she suggests that I hug myself nightly. This simple act has released the tension from my body (and my past) in a miraculous way. It has helped me to literally and figuratively "get a hold of myself."
—L. Nayer

## ☞ WHAT YOU NEED ☜

- A few minutes before bed
- Your imagination

# ⬤ *WHAT YOU DO* ⬤

Just before you go to sleep, focus on an image or a spot on the ceiling with your eyes open. Then, imagine a tranquil scene in nature. When you feel very sleepy, see yourself as a small child in a very fragile state. After you see yourself as a child, ask the adult you to pick up your child body. Hug yourself as a child and say some healing words. For example, "I love you. You are safe and healthy." If you do this every night, the child within you will feel loved and you as an adult will feel safer, happier, and healthier.

# The Family
# Meditation

*The heart at rest sees a feast in everything.*
—Asian Indian proverb

Whether we call it meditation, contemplative thought, or prayer, we can all experience the benefits of focused thought. When many people share this focus, the results can be very powerful. In his book *Healing Words*, Larry Dossey documents many studies of people with diseases whose health improved when people prayed for them, even when they didn't know them.

Many peoples of the world recognize that through prayer, dreams, and visions, individuals can touch the hearts and spirits of other human beings, regardless of time and distance. Imagine the power of family members adding love and insight to the equation. Listening through meditation is an important family practice that can help children learn to respect their inner lives and develop self-confidence.

## ⟣ WHAT YOU NEED ⟣

- *A quiet time when all can easily gather*
- *A comfortable place to sit*

## ⟣ WHAT YOU DO ⟣

*Pose a challenge or simply ask a question about a concern that the family shares. Is someone ill? Is the family contem-*

plating a move? Are there financial concerns that need solutions? Is there an unresolved conflict going on between family members?

Ask each person to sit quietly, focusing on the matter for 10 minutes in absolute silence. Then, ask each person to speak from the heart, sharing the insights gained. If no insights are forthcoming, continue the meditation that night in sleep and gather again the next day.

When we sit quietly with something, new sources of creativity become available as we learn to look to ourselves for answers.

# Mother's Candlelight Bath

*If you are not good for yourself, how can you be good for others? —Spanish proverb*

Water is wonderfully purifying and feels luxurious without costing much. After a full day responding to the needs of others, consider taking time for yourself, to relax and restore your body before sleep, once everyone is tucked in and no longer making demands of you.

## 🐟 WHAT YOU NEED 🐟

- *Bath salts or bubble bath*
- *A candle in a beautiful holder*
- *A loofah*
- *A plush towel or robe*
- *Scented body lotion*

## 🐟 WHAT YOU DO 🐟

Close the door after telling everyone it's mother's private time. Fill the tub high and pour in lots of bath salts or bubble bath—more than you need! Then, turn out the lights, light your candle, and watch the flame create rainbow colors in the bubbles.

Take a mental inventory of your day and think of all the people in it. Was there someone who wronged you? Was there an opportunity to help someone out that you declined? Are you feeling unfinished about a conversation with someone? Was something that you regret said in anger?

If you have a loofah, scrub yourself thoroughly in all the rough places, like the backs of your heels and elbows. With each stroke, name and release your negative feelings. For example, "I feel bad that I didn't offer to pick up my neighbor's child at school. She really needed the help today." Or, "I'm tired of yelling at the kids about leaving the house on time. Tomorrow, I will create a reward for getting it right, instead of screams for getting it wrong!"

As you name each event or feeling and scrub it away, think through and visualize how you would like the next exchange with that person to go. For example, you might offer to pick up your neighbor's child another day this week. Take three deep breaths after each new vision.

Once the negatives are handled, take three more deep breaths and think of the positive things that happened in your day. Should you be proud of an accomplishment that you may be discounting? Did you have a new insight today? Was it a beautiful day, a gray day, a holiday? Naming and celebrating the good things in our lives draws more of them to us.

Stay in the tub until you feel finished with this process and can hear yourself breathing deeply. Then, wrap yourself in your favorite towel or robe, rub a fragrant lotion like lilac or freesia into your arms and legs, and sleep well. Self-care helps you to remember that everyone you touch thrives when you do.

# Seeding Sweet Dreams

*I do not know whether I was then a man dreaming I was
a butterfly, or whether I am now a butterfly dreaming I
am a man. —Chuang Tse*

The end of the day can be the very best of times if you just take a
moment to bring the day to a peaceful close. Rather than fall into
bed exhausted, why not choose to get in bed 15 minutes sooner
to give yourself the chance for some really sweet dreams?

## 🐟 WHAT YOU NEED 🐟

- Flannel pajamas
- A candle in a holder
- A glass of water

## 🐟 WHAT YOU DO 🐟

First, put on the softest, friendliest pajamas you own. Sit
on the side of the bed, with both feet on the ground. Then, light
your candle and hold it in your hands.

Look into the flame and let it burn away any difficulties
in the day past. Then, turn your thoughts to the candle's illumi-
nating power and ask that your dreams shed light on any matters of concern to you. Take a sip of water after you have
asked your question. Then, blow out the candle and sleep. You
may have your answer sooner than you think.

# The Big Purge: Creating Space

*How many things I can do without!* —Socrates

When I prepared my house for sale, I purged, sending boxes and bags to charities, consignment stores, and starving students. The recipients were grateful, and my home has never been more peaceful. I didn't even know I had many of the things I was squirreling away. Lightening up helps us value what we really do love and keeps things moving through our lives. It creates the space for new people and new experiences to come into our lives.

In my new home, I have a ritual: When something new comes in, something old goes out. Even if it's just a magazine, when one comes in, one goes out. As YuWen outgrows a pair of shoes, she and I give them to a smaller friend or donate them to charity before new ones go into the closet. Moving things along keeps us from getting too attached to things that just end up weighing us down, mentally and physically. It frees us from the past and helps us develop more generous hearts. —V. Lang

## ● WHAT YOU NEED ●

- *A scheduled day once a quarter*
- *All family members*
- *A designated storage area*
- *Huge garbage bags*

## 🐟 WHAT YOU DO 🐟

At the start of each season, organize a purge day. Decide the rooms to be purged and the degree of purging desired. For example, are you going to remove surface clutter or are you really ready to open closets and drawers? Then, make an agreement to ask if anyone else in the family needs or wants an item you are purging. It saves tears later if you can remember that the old sweater from the 1960s, which you hate, is in style for your teenager.

Think about later use for some of the items. Is there a young adult who will set up housekeeping? If so, establish a storage area before you begin or you will just rotate things from place to place. If you have used women's business suits, consider giving them to Dress for Success, an organization that outfits low-income women for job interviews.

Evaluate each object to be purged by asking the question "Can I live happily without this?" If the answer is yes, take the item and, as you handle it, be aware of the use it had in your life, allowing yourself to feel whatever comes up. Then, when you feel ready, say, "With gratitude, I freely offer this for another's use." Put it in one of three bags—donation to charity, save for a student, or garbage.

# Peacemaking:
# A Weekly Family Meeting

*May it be delightful my house;*
*From my head may it be delightful;*
*To my feet may it be delightful;*
*Where I lie may it be delightful;*
*All above me may it be delightful;*
*All around me may it be delightful.*
—Navajo chant

At the Unitarian church a few years ago, our family learned about the "family meeting," and we have been meeting regularly ever since. When Sarah and Laura were younger, many of the issues that surfaced had to do with fairness. We had to test all of our peacemaking skills and remember that we are working together for the common good.

Whether you divide up chores, talk about the family budget, or discuss more serious issues, meeting as a family gives voice to both young and old and helps the household run smoothly.   —L. Nayer

## ❧ WHAT YOU NEED ❧

- A family meeting time once a week
- All members of the family present
- A family-meeting notebook
- A talking stick carved with the initials of each of the family members

## 🐟 WHAT YOU DO 🐟

Choose both a secretary and a leader, and rotate each week so eventually each person will do both jobs. Have the secretary date a page of the family-meeting notebook and record the concerns of each person.

Let each person who speaks hold the talking stick, a thick piece of wood carved with the initials of all family members. No one else is to talk except the person holding the stick. When the next person speaks, pass the stick to that person.

The leader should begin by saying what went well over the past week. Maybe the laundry got done on time, the older child cooked a meal, or there was a nice family outing to the park. Next, the leader should talk about what needs improvement—the plants were supposed to be watered, one person did most of the dog walking, or there was too much television over the weekend.

Each other person should then voice what went well and also state his concerns. During the time that each person talks, there is no interruption. After each person is finished, other family members may comment and come up with solutions. Maybe the job of watering the plants should be given to someone else. Perhaps a list of all the chores needs to be put up on the refrigerator. Perhaps a family outing should be planned for the next week as well.

It is important that this not be a put-down session and that no one person gets blamed. The family needs to be seen as a unit, with each person trying to help the others succeed.

At the end of the meeting, hang the talking stick on the wall in a prominent place for all to see. The notes may then be read at the next meeting by the new secretary.

# Welcoming a Stepchild

*When in the paling darkness of the lonely dawn you
stretch out your arms for your baby in the bed, I shall
say, "Baby is not there!"—Mother, I am going.*
—Rabindranath Tagore

For many years, my stepdaughter, Heather, came to our home
every Friday night for the weekend. It meant a complete change
of mode for all of us; she left the comfort and routine of her
mother's home and we shifted from two working professional
people to instant family. I wish I had thought to create a ritual
that would have let her know that we were happy to see her and
that she belonged with us just as much as she belonged in her
mother's home.   —V. Lang

## 🐟 WHAT YOU NEED 🐟

- *A fresh flower*
- *A family symbol*
- *A good chocolate*

## 🐟 WHAT YOU DO 🐟

*Just before your stepchild arrives, take time to think
about the visit from her perspective. She may feel off center,
miss friends, or be sad about leaving the other parent. Place a
small flower on her pillow, or, if you have a family symbol or
talisman (ours is a snail), put it on her pillow with her favorite
chocolate and turn down the bed hotel style.*

Each week, write a note from one or both of you to go along with the flower or symbol. It can be as simple as "We missed you." If there has been a sadness or a big event in the child's life, let the note reflect your understanding and willingness to talk if she wants to. She may want to keep a scrapbook of the notes or tack them to a bulletin board each week.

# The Family
# Time-Out

*All happy families resemble one another, but each
unhappy family is unhappy in its own way.*
—Leo Tolstoy

Perhaps the happiest families are the ones that approach the
challenges of family life with humor. In my family, for example,
I am trying to balance the needs of a 52-year-old man, a
menopausal mom, a 4-year-old preschooler, and a college
student!

In blended families like ours, the varying ages and experience levels of the family members can present huge challenges.
We all need time out from the expectations and compromises
required in family life, especially in families with independent
souls and teens. As my dear friend Ellen likes to say, "Do we have
to be joined at the hip to be a good family?"   —V. Lang

## ◗ WHAT YOU NEED ◖

- A family free day
- A set-up day to make it work

## ◗ WHAT YOU DO ◖

Decide on a date that works for everyone. Set guidelines
appropriate for your family. For example: Each person is free
to get out of bed, eat, drink, dress, nap, talk on the phone, and

come and go without any questions asked. If a child misses a class or practice, he must get permission or make it up. If a parent sleeps in, someone else gets breakfast. If a teenager talks on the phone for more than 30 minutes, he must be sure others don't need to call out. Each person cleans up his own mess.

The idea is, with common decency in mind, each person is free to think of himself first for one full day.

Be sure to think through the necessary set-up. Get groceries in the house, lay the soccer shoes by the door, get someone else to drive the carpool, whatever it takes to make the day run smoothly. If there is an elder to care for, consider a respite-care program; many communities now have them.

Later, at a family supper, discuss what worked, what didn't, and what was learned. If this was a good practice, make it a monthly ritual.

# Family Stories

*Because the tale of how we suffer, how we are delighted,*
*and how we may triumph is never new, it must always*
*be heard. There isn't any other tale to tell, it's the only*
*light we've got in all this darkness. —James Baldwin*

Mary Pipher, author of *Reviving Ophelia*, has done significant work with adolescents about their sense of identity. One of the things she talks about is the necessity of family stories.

Many of us grow up distanced from relatives, or we believe that what happened in the past is not important. But, if we are to feel a part of the long thread of humankind, what Uncle Fred did in 1929 or Aunt Katherine saw as a nurse in World War II all make up a distinctive family portrait. If these stories are used for enlightenment and told with wisdom, they can draw families together through the ancient art of storytelling. This ritual can also be done with a group of friends who have been together a long time and have many stories to share.

## ⬤ WHAT YOU NEED ⬤

- The family gathered together
- A guide for the evening (this can rotate; children can guide as well)
- Pens, crayons, and markers
- A family storybook
- A tape recorder

# 🐟 WHAT YOU DO 🐟

Pick one night each month or each season to be Family Story Night. If you have a fireplace and it's cold, throw on a log. Serve cocoa, tea, or coffee and sit in the living room or around a table. Turn off the lights to create a calm atmosphere, and light a candle. In summer, you may want to sit outdoors under the stars, around a campfire.

The guide should begin with either the eldest or youngest and ask each person to tell a personal story about the past. The stories may be embellished but should stay true to the events. Young children may recount stories of when they were three or four.

At the end of the evening, the guide may ask everyone to write his story in the Family Story Book or simply record the evening on tape. The taped voices of a loved grandmother or a special uncle are a treasure, particularly cherished after they die.

For those who prefer to create a visual memory, include drawings, pictures, or photos in the book.

# The Bosworth Café: Expression Night at Home

*We are all attached*
*like tiny red and white carnations*
*whose stems touch*
*at the bottom of glass.*
*—Louise Nayer*

Growing up in Greenwich Village and later becoming a poet, I have always had a house full of artists and writers. I moved to San Francisco to be part of the poetry community, immersing myself in workshops and readings. Over the past 15 years, working full time as an English instructor and raising children, I have found myself going to readings less and losing some of that inspired and magical community that gave me so much.

In an attempt to bring more creativity into our life, my family has started a monthly gathering at our home on Bosworth Street where both seasoned artists and novices can share their work. I have always believed that everyone is an artist, so no one is turned away! We have had demonstrations of sculptures made from lemons and oranges, piano recitals, poetry and prose readings as well as an exhibition of computer calendar art.

As people become increasingly fatigued from the pressures of work, this monthly gathering adds magic to the month. I have been surprised and pleased at how many people ask, "When is the next Bosworth Café Night?" and how excited they get about practicing a piece on the piano or learning a new song to sing.   —L. Nayer

## 🐟 WHAT YOU NEED 🐟

- Invitations with dates for 6 months
- Food and drink brought by everyone

## 🐟 WHAT YOU DO 🐟

Send out flyers marked with dates for the next 6 months so people can put the dates on their calendars. You can make a Café Night logo or an unusual flyer using your street name.

When people arrive, serve the food and drink. Afterward, sit in a circle in the living room. Ask one guest (a different person each time) to bring a poem, a passage from a book, or a song to begin the evening. It can be something written for the occasion or a favorite song or poem.

Then, begin the sharing time. Keep the performances to 10 minutes per person so people will want to return to the next gathering. Encourage each other, whether the person is a first-time poet or a widely published author. This is a time to gather together and to remember that the creative spirit lives in all of us. End the gathering by holding hands and passing a squeeze, each person focusing on the beauty of what has been presented that night.

# Virtual Shopping

*I cannot and will not cut my conscience to fit this
year's fashions. —Lillian Hellman*

When I am bored, I shop. I don't particularly need anything or
want anything; I just like to look and touch and handle things.
Once I buy something and take it home, it often loses its fascination for me.

Now that I realize this about myself, I go "virtual shopping" now and then. I take YuWen along and we go into a store
on a treasure hunt. I ask her what the most special item is, or the
most beautiful color, or the oddest-looking thing. We make
shopping a looking-and-seeing adventure, and then we leave.
If something that I really want sticks in my mind the next day, I
go back. I like to think this is teaching my daughter to be able to
appreciate things without having to own them. In a world
where so many people are still living at subsistence level, do we
really need all the trinkets, the fashions, and the fixes that sweep
our culture?   —V. Lang

## WHAT YOU NEED

- *A shopping destination*
- *Someone to go treasure hunting with you*

## WHAT YOU DO

As you shop, let yourself see and describe everything that
is beautiful to you. What is the most memorable object, dress,

lamp? What is the best example of forest green? What objects are perfectly suited to someone else in your life? Make notes for birthday or Christmas use. Compare your thoughts with the other person; it is fascinating to get a child's perspective or that of a friend who may have an excellent sense of taste.

If you are a catalogue shopper, circle every item you like in the catalogue as if you were going to call to buy it. Then, go back and draw double circles around your favorite two items. Lay the catalogue aside; if you wake up the next day truly wanting one of the items for yourself or someone else and can afford it, then make the call. But you may find you have already had your fun.

# Driving Miss Daisy: A Grandmother/ Granddaughter Day

### Grandmother

*I hadn't asked her much, just how she felt,*
*and she told me all about her day,*
*and how she's washed the sheets,*
*how she could not understand*
*why the towel got so heavy*
*when it was wet.*
*She'd also sunned the mattresses, such tired bones and*
*so much to do,*
*and my eyes filled with tears*
*when I thought of how I was simply*
*going to say 'Salaam' and walk away*
*and so many words would have been*
*trapped inside her.*
*I would have passed by as if*
*what lay between those bedclothes*
*was just old life*
*and not really my grandmother.*
*—Sameeneh Shirazie*

When I visit my Aunt Margaret, now 95, we have coffee and lament the hotel-like nature of assisted living. With everything done for her, she has come to feel unnecessary in her own life. The bed is made, the meals are prepared, and her social life is organized. There is simply nothing left for her to do. Gone are the little things that gave life meaning—making her bed the way she likes it, driving a car, baking cookies, squeezing a grape at the grocery, and dusting her beautiful china. Now, it's coffee in mugs with a corporate logo and the kind but unfamiliar faces.

I believe the assumption that most older people want everything done for them is wrong. There is so much loss when an elder gives up a loved home. It is a double blow to give up autonomy, too. Here is a ritual anyone can do for an older loved one who has lost their freedom.   —V. Lang

## WHAT YOU NEED

- An afternoon date once a month
- A car
- A wheelchair or walker, if necessary
- Patience

## WHAT YOU DO

Offer to pick up your grandmother for a tag-along afternoon, just your usual errands and routine. If walking is difficult or impossible for her, go to a grocery that has special carts with rumble seats (many large stores now have them) or take along a wheelchair. As you go up and down the aisles, put oranges and basil, fresh coffee, and other fragrant foods in her hands so she can feel and smell them. Offer to purchase special items she can no longer get in assisted living, like Cocoa Puffs, baby carrots, pink grapefruit, even old favorites like shoelace licorice. Go slowly enough for her to really take in the experience and look at all the new products she's never seen.

Continue on your errands to pick up a child, drop off mail, whatever you ordinarily do, involving her whenever possible. Cook her a dinner from the groceries you bought together, and let her dry dishes sitting down. Make a date to do this once a month, so she knows it's coming up and can look forward to it. You will share memorable days together just being yourselves.

# The "No Place Special" Day

*Life is what happens to you while you're making other plans. —John Lennon*

One of the nicest days in my life was one that went haywire. A babysitter cancellation meant a complete change of work plans, and YuWen and I were in free fall until I caught myself and decided to just go with the day. We strolled, window-shopped, bought groceries, and read books at the library, just going with the flow. Over root beer floats, she turned to me and said, "Mama, this is the best day of my life."

Instead of my usual preoccupation with time, school, and agendas, I was present and able to just be with her, no goals, no destination, no shoulds. She got to decide what we did next, and I got to see the world through her magical eyes. Louise told me her mother used to do something like this when she was young. The two of them would get in the car and her mom would say, "Let's get lost." It is important to allow for spontaneity in our competitive culture and to let our children be children.   —V. Lang

## ☙ WHAT YOU NEED ❧

- An unplanned day with your child once a month
- An agreement that both of you get to pick what to do

## WHAT YOU DO

Set off on foot or by car without any idea where you're going. Ask your child for ideas on where to go and what to do as the day progresses. Avoid planning anything, just let yourself go. Children seldom get to create their own day from scratch and will love the chance to take the lead without being told, "Time for this or time for that." In our overly programmed world, "no place special" days are golden.

# Seeing Green: Learning to Look

*This is how a human being can change:*
*there's a worm addicted to eating*
*grape leaves.*
*Suddenly, he wakes up,*
*call it grace, whatever, something*
*wakes him, and he's no longer*
*a worm.*
*He's the entire vineyard,*
*and the orchard too, the fruit, the trunks,*
*a growing wisdom and joy*
*that doesn't need to devour.*
—Rumi (translated by Coleman Barks)

One day, our family went exploring in the tide pools of Morro Bay with our friends the Maruzka family. Katy Maruzka and YuWen started to collect shells and rocks, bits of kelp, and driftwood. As they brought their treasures back to the blanket, I began to look closely at the colors, counting at least a dozen different subtle shades of green, from beach-glass jade to deep spinach. The three of us made it a game to keep finding green and presented our "study in green" to Katy's mom, who is a gifted artist.

Afterward, when I thought about that day, I realized how life becomes an exercise in how we see. Before, if someone had asked me what color the ocean is, would I have said, "A study in green"?

The ability to see and to keep seeing with fresh eyes is critical in a world that seeks to label, define, and limit. Here is a ritual that allows us and our young children to learn to see.   —V. Lang

## 🐟 WHAT YOU NEED 🐟

- An afternoon once a week
- A place in nature (ocean, woods, a local park, or your own yard)

## 🐟 WHAT YOU DO 🐟

Pick a destination and ask your child to go on a hunt with you to make a collection of all the interesting things you can find in nature—feathers in a yard, polished rocks in a riverbed, unusual leaves in a forest, beach glass at the ocean. Lay out your treasures and examine them together, grouping them by color, texture, or size.

Give creative names to all the subtle shades—robin's-egg blue, blood-orange red—respecting each person's unique perception of color. Some days, you may prefer to make it a study in shapes. Each day you do this, take home one souvenir of your study, and label and date it as a record of that day's study.

# The Men's Group: Deepening Boyhood Bonds

*Whereas nature turns girls into women, society has to turn boys into men. —Anthony Stevens*

I love to watch boys at play. One of my favorite movies is *Stand By Me*, a high-adventure story full of blood and guts, humor and pathos. The boys encounter a pond of leeches, a runaway train, a dead body, and the meaning of friendship.

My husband laments the absence of simple boyhood joys in his life. In his work in the corporate world, he is typically confronted with men whose competitive outlook prevents true connection. He longs for a place to share his deepest thoughts and feelings with other men but finds few opportunities to do so.   —V. Lang

## 🐟 WHAT YOU NEED 🐟

- *A day off from family and work responsibilities*
- *A small group of male friends*
- *An exciting place to be together*
- *A supportive spouse*

## 🐟 WHAT YOU DO 🐟

Pick an activity your male friends can all do or want to try. Go whitewater rafting, climb a mountain, go on a safari, whatever appeals to the group and fits the budget. The goal is to pick something exciting, new, and full of adventure.

Spend at least 1 full day together. That night, share a meal that all help prepare. Shop, cook, eat, and clean up without any outside help. After dinner, gather by a campfire or fireplace and throw out a topic that concerns everyone present. It might be the fears of new fatherhood, how to handle a strong-willed teenager, or a humorous topic like "What do women really want?" Agree that everything will be said in confidence, and give everyone a chance to speak without judgment. If this is a good experience, make it a monthly ritual.

As the men's group grows and develops, this circle of men can support each other as a "virtual village," providing counsel and support for their sons and daughters as the children reach adolescence.

# Befriending an Animal

*It is in the tiniest acts, the ones that no one sees, that
we express who we are. —Virginia Lang*

I once found a tiny mole dying on a patch of green grass. His
little chest was pounding hard, and death was near. I was car-
rying a bottle of spring water, so I poured it on him and then
placed him on a leaf. In the past, I would have walked by him,
focused on more important things, self-conscious and certain
that to stop was impractical or silly. But this time, as I watched
his tiny chest rise and fall, I felt connected to this fragile life,
seeing him as an equal the way children do.

Charles Darwin wrote, "Animals, whom we have made our
slaves, we do not like to consider our equal." When we ignore
or neglect an animal, we are really saying, "We are superior to
you, so we don't have to care." This mindset of domination of
animals and nature harms the Earth and violates our souls. We
must help each other to care.   —V. Lang

## 🐟 WHAT YOU NEED 🐟

- *An animal wounded or in distress*
- *The phone number of the Humane Society in your area*

## 🐟 WHAT YOU DO 🐟

*The next time you see an animal in distress, offer what-
ever help you safely can. Be careful to assess the situation,
being mindful of the risk of infection and your effect on the an-*

imal. Well-intentioned people have been hurt or have caused wounded animals, frightened by the approach of humans, to run into traffic.

If the animal is dead, take the time to bury or move it to a safe place in a simple, respectful manner. You may want to use a leaf or two sticks to lift a small animal if it has started to decompose. If you are unsure of what to do or need help, call the Humane Society in your area.

The Humane Society of the United States estimates that more than a million animals are killed on the road every day, and several million more are wounded and die off the road. Make it a daily practice to brake for animals and to drive with care.

# BEGINNINGS

*Beginnings: seeds in the ground, new forms created, able to take root. The cry of a new baby, with its planetary eyes and moon-shaped head; the journey of new parents to keep their love for each other alive; the hopes that live on the threshold of a first home.*

*Our lives are filled with beginnings—being brought into the life of a family, beginning life in a new place, or simply beginning the day in a newly conscious way. When we begin something, we have the opportunity to bring awareness to our beliefs and assumptions, to challenge ourselves to be new, different, better.*

# Breaking the Mold: Beginning a More Creative Life

*Only the dreamer can change the dream.*
—*John Logan*

Everyone has creative abilities, but few of us continue to discover and develop our talents as adults. For many years, I worked as a poet-in-residence at senior centers and nursing homes and was constantly amazed by the poems written by people who had never written poetry before in their lives.

One woman, who had Alzheimer's disease, wrote about her childhood in Chicago, where she danced on polished wooden floors surrounded by floor-length mirrors. I felt as if I were with her in that dance studio. I also worked with a woman who was already accomplished as a therapist and speaker in Europe. She chose to live a creative life in San Francisco, produced two poetry books, and is now a well-known painter in both Europe and the United States. She is also blind.

We are all creative, but it often takes the right people and the right moments in our lives to let us create. Between family responsibilities, paying bills, and working, few of us get the chance to explore our creative sides. But art can actually save lives. I have seen it many times in my work when people have been allowed to express their deepest feelings in a refreshing way without being judged or criticized. Here is a ritual that can help you break the mold and see yourself as a creative person.   —L. Nayer

## 🐟 WHAT YOU NEED 🐟

- The necessary tools of your craft
- The same time set aside each week as your creative time, at least 2 to 3 hours
- A room where you can be alone or a place to make your art

## 🐟 WHAT YOU DO 🐟

Make sure you have the tools of the trade. You can go on a shopping spree before your first creative date with yourself and buy art supplies, paper or a journal book, a camera, clay, or whatever you need. Make sure you have enough material to last for a while, so you don't use a lack of supplies as an excuse to not create.

Finish ahead of time any work you need to do for your job or family, so your creative time is kept sacred. Notify family and friends that a certain time of day or night is *your* time. People are not to ask you out to dinner or to the movies and are not even to call during that time unless it is an emergency.

When you begin, suspend all judgment and criticism. Perhaps you *will* eventually be a famous writer, paid handsomely for your work, but what matters now is that you are creating something you love. You may choose to share your work with loving friends, but keep in mind that early criticism can be paralyzing. After a few months of doing your work, you may be surprised at how much better you feel about yourself and the world. This is only the beginning. Who knows where it will lead?

# Blessing Hunting: Beginning to See What's Good

*If the only prayer you say in your whole life is "thank you," that would suffice. —Meister Eckhart*

Do you ever find yourself screaming at the television or punching the newspaper? Do you rail at the world as a daily practice? I did. I was growing cynical and sad watching man's latest expression of inhumanity. I wasn't often thankful anymore, and I didn't see much that was good.

Then, I realized that nothing that I heard or read was from my direct experience. It was all secondhand, filtered through the eyes of someone else. Without the balance of my own eyes, my own experience, I was dwelling on secondhand accounts of murders, rapes, fires, and every other kind of human atrocity. Was there nothing good going on?

When you expose yourself to too much bad, you eventually stop seeing any good. You start to think of the world as the thousands of ways we hurt one another. Theologian Matthew Fox suggests, "We must go blessing hunting because our culture is so steeped in cynicism and despair . . . that we have lost our awareness and even *curiosity* about what is good." —V. Lang

## ✒ WHAT YOU NEED ✒

- Time in a quiet place
- Matthew Fox's List of Awesome Things

## ✒ WHAT YOU DO ✒

Give yourself a 1-week break from the news. In this week, take the time you would have spent reading the paper or watching television to take a walk and be with a friend in nature. Make a point to go blessing hunting. For a start, simply sit and reflect on these incredible thoughts from *Sins of the Spirit, Blessing of the Flesh* by Matthew Fox.

### A List of Awesome Things

- In a single season, a large elm tree makes about six million leaves.
- Squashes have been measured to exert a lifting force of 5,000 pounds per square inch.
- For every particle of matter there are one billion particles of light.
- Every single hydrogen atom in our bodies was once part of the Big Bang itself.
- Blood evolved directly from ancient seawater.
- In a lifetime, a heart beats about four billion times.
- With every breath, we inhale millions of molecules of sky.
- African Bushmen can see four moons of Jupiter with the naked eye.
- Dogs and cats have adopted orphaned skunks or piglets.
- Year-old beavers help their parents take care of younger siblings.
- One female ocean sunfish carried 300 million eggs.

Every day, write down just five things that were good. When a week is up, make a decision about how, when, and in what ways you wish to take in information. You may want to listen to foreign news like that from the British Broadcasting Corporation and seek out less commercial sources of information, like National Public Radio and public television. I like to read *The New York Times'* Sunday edition. Remember to balance what you take from outside sources with your own knowing, and cultivate your ability to see blessings.

# Waiting to Adopt: Beginning a Heart Connection

*When your heart speaks, take good notes.*
*—Panna Flower*

In the months of waiting to adopt a baby from China, I was overwhelmed with every possible emotion. It was hard enough to wait, but the not knowing was excruciating. I craved that elemental tie that birth mothers feel in their bodies, a cord that would tie me to this faraway child who was on the Earth but as yet unknown to me.

One day, I received word from our translator, Xiao Ching, that a picture of our child had arrived. My husband, Dean, and I leaped into the car to go and get it. What we got was a postage stamp–size picture, just the face of a small infant in a red quilted jacket, and the news that she was from Hunan province. Though it wasn't much, it made her real. I started to write to her and began a "conversation" that gave me great comfort in the days of waiting to go to China. When we finally met, I felt as if I had always known her.

Louise told me that my dreams and fears during this time were much like her own when she was waiting for Sarah and Laura to be born. I was becoming a mother every day of the wait, bonding to my child in my heart.   —V. Lang

## 🐟 WHAT YOU NEED 🐟

- Time alone
- A place to write, draw, or just sit in silence

## 🐟 WHAT YOU DO 🐟

During the long days of waiting, take time to simply sit in silence for a few minutes each day, letting your heart slowly embrace your waiting child. Contemplate the thought that you are already a mother; your child is simply away from home.

If you have a picture of the child you are to adopt, make an enlarged color copy of it and place it somewhere you can see it. Write short messages to her and attach them to the picture. If you like to write, try a poem or a love letter. If you are more visual, draw or sculpt something for her that expresses the essence of her as you see it in the picture. It will be a precious keepsake later.

Here is a poem I wrote for YuWen that really helped me make a connection to her.

### Waiting for My Daughter
### (for YuWen)

My heart sings out with longing for you,
good luck girl of the Hunan winter.
White moonbeam fingers stroke your sleeping head,
sculpt your pink ears, trace your butter brown lips.
My heart knows you China girl of black night
in the red Changsha coals that warm your small feet.
It throws a rope wide across the brave clouds,
loops your dragon soul in soft cords of love.
My heart can see you Mao's girl of no name.

It names you with salt tears that fall from my eyes.
Its long gaze embraces your strong blue-veined skull,
enfolds your soft body in long arms of hope.
My heart sings to you, puts you to sleep—
to the thunder of hummingbirds batting their wings:
their columbine nectar perfumes your sweet bed,
their gray velvet heads guard your slow, sleeping breath.
My heart awaits you, girl of ripe dreams:
the fruit will soon fall, the skin will peel open.
Come take your place in the womb of my heart:
in the mile-deep hollow of my waiting heart.

# Loving Hands
# for a Mother-to-Be

*With a child just an eyedrop away*
*I am the egg being timed*
*the round belly of the moon*
*the biggest house of all.*
*—Louise Nayer*

When a woman gives birth for the first time, life changes overnight. A couple is now three and many adjustments are made to welcome a new baby into the new world. But the actual changes start much earlier in the woman's body and heart.

I know that when I was pregnant, I was more protective of myself, just as in a number of months I would be protective of the new life outside me. My husband and I discussed finances and room changes and purchased basics for the baby-to-be. There was also fear: Would everything go all right? Would the labor be long and hard? Would the baby be healthy? Would this world be too harsh for our innocent newcomer?

Many women have strange dreams during pregnancy. I dreamt that my baby was a small black line that ran away from me in the grass. I couldn't find her and woke up sweating. Women are often afraid but don't discuss their fears. To go along with good prenatal care and regular checkups, here is a ritual that can help a pregnant woman relax and feel taken care of during one of the most vulnerable times in her life. So much of a pregnancy is spent thinking about the baby; it is good to have at least 1 hour a week just for the mother.   —L. Nayer

## 🐟 WHAT YOU NEED 🐟

- A pregnant woman
- Her best friend or mate
- A small gift such as flowers or a bar of jasmine soap
- A glass of water with a twist of lemon
- Some scented oil (lavender is nice)
- A journal

## 🐟 WHAT YOU DO 🐟

Set aside 1 hour once a week for gentle massage of the expectant mother's head, shoulders, hands, legs, and feet. Make sure to make an appointment and keep it! Treat the woman like royalty as she lies down in her favorite spot, wearing loose-fitting clothes. Offer your gift.

After offering the lemon water and finding a comfortable position for her, start by gently massaging her feet with the oil. As you massage, let her know she is free to talk or simply to feel the loving hands helping her relax. Maybe she wants to cry, laugh, yawn, or simply lie still. She might not talk much during the first two or three sessions, but later she might find that this is a good time to let out feelings about the upcoming birth. Listen to her and let her know that she is safe.

End the session with a hug and a promise to massage her next week. If she wants, she can write in her journal for a short time after the massage and keep it as a diary of her feelings during this spectacular time in her life.

# New Mother: The First Week after Giving Birth

*Let me rest and drink in this moment,*
*as you lay beside me, this sweet separation.*
*—Virginia Lang*

I have a friend, Rae Ling Chang, who is a thoroughly modern woman. Raised in Taiwan and educated in this country, she nonetheless chose to observe Chinese tradition when she had her babies. She was expected to stay in her home for a full month. She was not to shower, to walk down steps, or to expose herself to cold wind. Her mother fed her restorative soups and cared for the newborn while she regained her strength.

Most of my American friends delivered their babies in sterile hospital operating rooms or birthing rooms. They were discharged the same or the next day and back to work in a matter of weeks. No one had her mother present.

Giving birth is one of the high points in a woman's life, a fragile, tender time unlike any other. Why do we rush through it as if it were only a medical event? Where is the celebration and regard for the woman who has just brought a new life into the world?  —V. Lang

## ➤ WHAT YOU NEED ➤

- *A mother's helper*
- *A list of your favorite foods, scents, poems, and music*

## ❧ WHAT YOU DO ❧

During the long days of waiting, develop a picture of yourself in the days after giving birth. Where are you sitting; what are you eating; what objects of beauty are in the room; who is there? Make a list of special items you would really enjoy.

Next, ask a special person—your mother, best friend, or sister—to be your mother's helper and to stay with you as much as possible the week the baby comes home. In this culture, we are hesitant to ask for help, so ask this directly as a special request and spell out the ways you would like help. A month or so before the baby is due, take your helper on a special trip to buy some things that will make these first weeks home comfortable for you. Consider items like:

- A special down pillow
- Favorite soups to have on hand
- Scented soaps and a loofah for the bath
- Very soft slippers and feminine pajamas
- A book of poetry by Mary Oliver
- Carol Rosenberger's beautiful ... *Perchance to Dream: A Lullaby Album for Children and Adults*

Celebrate yourself in whatever ways your taste and circumstances allow.

# Waiting for a Sister or Brother

*Serenity*
*When I am singing to you*
*on earth all evil ends*
*—Gabriela Mistral*

As a younger child surrounded by people who were firstborns, I had little understanding of the experience of being a big brother/big sister until my older daughter, Sarah, became an older sibling. We read her a book, *I Want to Tell You about My Baby*, that helped tremendously. We also talked to her often during the pregnancy to ease the transition. She even talked to my tummy and began her own relationship with her sister-to-be. Though my children fight at times, I am happy that their relationship has been an unusually close one.

My sister told me about an older boy who sang to his pregnant mom for many months. The baby loved the song "You Are My Sunshine." The mom said the baby moved back and forth in her tummy when the little boy sang.

Sadly, after the baby girl was born, she was very ill. The nurses told the parents she might die. The little boy kept insisting he wanted to sing to his baby, but no one would let him into the hospital nursery. Out of desperation and wanting to please their son, the parents finally got clearance; and the little boy, only 3 years old, sang to his dying sister.

He sang many times, and her body began to stir. A few days later, she began to recover. Was it his singing? Perhaps.   —L. Nayer

## ☛ WHAT YOU NEED ☚

- A pregnant mother
- An older child
- A special song the child picks to sing

## ☛ WHAT YOU DO ☚

When you have told the older child of the pregnancy, have him sing a special song to the baby as often as possible. This can also be snuggle time for the older sibling. The song can be made up or one the child knows from school or home.

After the baby is born, print out the words to the song on a sheet of colored paper. Have the child decorate it. Take a picture of the child and baby and frame the song and picture. Place the song and framed picture over the older child's bed.

# Still Precious: Special Time for an Older Child

*You are the universe: the sun, the sky, the moon. Let me see your hands, like no other's, the way the lines are deep, the way they curve, like no other's. —Louise Nayer*

When my daughter Laura was born, we gave my older daughter, Sarah, a table and chairs and signed the gift from Laura. Sarah was thrilled—and even more thrilled when friends came and took her to the zoo and out for ice cream. Often when a baby is born, the older child or children need to feel included and that they are still precious beings. It is important that very close friends and family remember the older child by bringing small gifts. Sometimes, these gifts can be brought to the baby shower; at other times, handed to the older child on a separate occasion.

Think about your older child, what she likes to do, her favorite places to visit, her favorite foods. She will be thrilled to go out for a milkshake with mom, dad, or a trusted adult once a week. Keep the attention focused on your child—no phones or reading the paper. Even if the child says nothing but simply enjoys scooping the whipped cream off the milkshake and knowing you are there, that is enough.   —L. Nayer

## WHAT YOU NEED

- *Special time set aside*
- *A calendar picked out by your older child*

## ✦ WHAT YOU DO ✦

Near the time of the delivery, family and close friends can take the older child aside and make some dates on a calendar. Everyone can find 1 to 2 hours during the first month after the baby is born. Perhaps a trip can be taken to the zoo or a walk down the street for an ice-cream cone. It doesn't have to take a lot of time or money, but these special moments can be an opportunity for the older child to have time away from the busy household and to get some extra attention.

Parents can also make dates; the mom can do this when she feels stronger, so the child can look forward to special time with mom and dad as well. Some families continue the once-a-week or once-every-2-weeks ritual with each child. It helps each child feel loved and reduces sibling rivalry!

# Beginning as Parents: Learning From the Past

*The lines on your hand stop and start like pilgrimages.*
*—Louise Nayer*

My father loves language and poetry. I remember him reading Shakespeare to me when I was young and endlessly reciting Keats: "The beaded bubbles winking at the brim." This inspired my own writing.

My mother was always organized and forever practical. I rebelled against her practicality for many years, but I now fully appreciate what she taught me.

One way to think about how we want to parent our own children is to reflect on how our parents and the important adults in our lives enriched us and helped as evolve into full human beings. Here is a ritual to help expectant mothers and fathers make conscious choices about what they want to pass on to the next generation. —L. Nayer

## 🐟 WHAT YOU NEED 🐟

- *A dinner-table conversation once a week before a baby is born or before a child enters a home through adoption*

- Photos of memorable times in your childhood with a parent or favorite adult
- An agreement to focus on parenting

## 🐟 WHAT YOU DO 🐟

Think about specific people from your childhood and what they did that helped you grow and made you happy. Perhaps your mom ordered all your favorite food at a restaurant and then told you how beautiful you looked, or your dad read poetry to you before bed. Specific aunts, uncles, or family friends may have played a role in your life, taught you about art, showed you how to jump the waves beyond the breakers, or simply sat with you and let you talk about your day. What do these moments have in common? How can you recreate these moments for your own child?

During one or more of the conversations, contemplate a photograph of an adult who was special to you. What qualities did that person possess? What is it you can learn from her life? Perhaps one person taught you courage, another gave you many compliments and made you feel good about yourself, a teacher opened you up to the vast world of art and literature, or a grandfather listened to you when it seemed everyone else was too busy.

If you wish, write down the names of specific people and the qualities that were important to you. You can create a collage of photos and words and reflect on it as you become a mom and dad.

# Beginning Life in a New Home

*Home is the place where when you go there,*
*They have to take you in.*
*—Robert Frost*

When we bought our home in Wallingford, Pennsylvania, we learned that only two families had owned it in 85 years: John and Sarah Albert's family and Dr. Donald and Nancy Patterson's family. When we moved in, I felt the presence of these families and so many other people here in this home we were now to occupy. Children were born here, cats and dogs were raised here, friends were welcomed here, elders died here. The place was vibrating with memories, both good and bad.

We had spent so long working out the details of the sale—the finances, the title insurance, the mortgage, the escrow terms—that we had given very little time to the actual feelings that came up in the handing over of the home from the Patterson family to ours. I began to feel better after writing to Dr. Patterson (his wife, Nancy, had died) and telling him how excited we were about the house he had loved and lived in happily for 30 years. He wrote back to tell me how pleased he was that I loved it too.

The night after we moved in, I sat in front of the first fire we lit in the hearth and "talked" to Sarah Albert and Nancy Patterson. I told them I would be taking care of the house now but would always honor their memories here. As I finished speaking, a large log split open and fell with a huge burst of light emanating from its middle.

Wherever you choose to live, someone has been there before, someone who called the place home. Here is a ritual to honor the space of others and all the memories that fill a space.   —V. Lang

## ➤ WHAT YOU NEED ➤

- The first night in a new home or apartment
- A fireplace or a scented candle

## ➤ WHAT YOU DO ➤

Light a fire or the candle and sit quietly, thinking about the people who have lived in the home before. If you have a photograph of them, hold it in your hand.

Say silently or aloud, "I accept responsibility for the care of this home and will honor the memories of all those who have lived here before me. May this home be a place of happiness and peace."

If you are the first to occupy a new home, you might say, "I am grateful for the many hands that built this home, and I now accept responsibility for its care. May this home be a place of happiness and peace."

# Beginning to Serve Yourself

*Alone now, I can hear bells from a far-off village*
*where an old woman bathes me in light from her eyes.*
*"Eat well," she says, stroking my long hair and*
*handing me warm bread and honey. "Fill your body*
*with nourishment, with light." —Louise Nayer*

Most of us have loved and lost and at some time in our lives felt overwhelming grief and loneliness. We think, "Will I ever get over these feelings? Will I be alone now forever?" Friends tell us of the support groups at church, new classes at college. They encourage us with well-meaning suggestions "to get out and smell the roses" and that "there are more fish in the sea."

Though it is important to get out and live life again, it is equally important to experience our grief and to slow down, take a deep breath, and take care of ourselves, whatever life holds for us. For many of us who have been serving others, it is crucial that we learn how to care for ourselves.

## ◖● WHAT YOU NEED ●◗

- Soothing music
- Your favorite food for a meal (you may want to pick out a new recipe that looks especially appealing)
- A decorative place mat and linen napkin
- Utensils
- A wine glass (for wine or any drink you choose)
- A candle

## ⬗ WHAT YOU DO ⬖

While the soothing music plays, prepare the meal for yourself with patience and love. Thoughts of sadness or "Why am I cooking if it's for just myself?" might surface, but push them away with thoughts of "I'm taking good care of myself." Set the table with the place mat, linen napkin, utensils, and wine glass. When the meal is ready, take it to the table and pour your drink. Light the candle and take a deep breath, saying, "I'm happy to be taking care of myself so well. I deserve the best!"

# FABULOUS
# FIRSTS

First steps, first school, first job, first kiss: We can never again capture the excitement, the range of emotion, the sheer drama of the firsts in our lives. And yet it is so easy to overlook these poignant moments, to let them go unremarked, uncelebrated.

With just a little thought, we can frame these moments in ceremony, preserving their uniqueness in our memories like wild violets pressed in an old, dog-eared book.

# First Day of School for a Preschooler

*When the first baby laughed for the first time,*
*the laugh broke into a thousand pieces and they all*
*went skipping about, and that was the beginning*
*of fairies.* —Peter Pan *by J. M. Barrie*

What is more precious than the laughter of a child, the total abandon and head-flinging joy of pure glee? The first few years in the life of a child are so magical and so special that it can be heart wrenching to leave this time behind for the more practical, socialized world of school.

On YuWen's first day of preschool, Dean and I went with her, holding her hand and trying desperately not to look at one another as our eyes welled up with tears. As much as we liked Montessori Children's House, we knew this entry into the "real" world would slowly move her from her magical life to one of limits, rules, and realities. We just weren't ready. Is anyone?   —V. Lang

## ☞ WHAT YOU NEED ☜

- *Time to transition*
- *A soft felt heart cut in two irregular pieces*

## ☞ WHAT YOU DO ☜

*First, be certain to give yourself enough time to spend 10 to 20 minutes of transition time at your child's school. For many* days after YuWen started school, she would say, "Will you get me started?" After a short game or puzzle, she would be ready to join in with others.

Once you see that your child is able to make this transition, tell her to look in her pocket for a small piece of felt that is soft and has a message from you on it. "I am with you in my heart" is a good one. Show her that you have the other half of the heart in *your* pocket, and tell her that you will always return to complete the heart every day. When you pick her up, match the hearts together and let her see that you have been missing her just as much as she has been missing you.

# First Day Back to School

A colleague of mine at City College of San Francisco told me about this simple ritual that she does each year with her children. At the beginning of the summer, she plants her garden. At the end of the summer, when the garden is in full bloom and the children are beginning school, she snaps a photo of each of her children by a favorite apple tree on the first day of school. The family can measure how the children have grown by how tall they are next to the tree. Just as the garden grows throughout the summer, the children are part of nature, growing and blossoming in their own ways. This is a way of commemorating the first day of school.   —L. Nayer

## 🐟 WHAT YOU NEED 🐟

- A backyard or outdoor site for snapping photos
- A camera
- Something from the garden
- A photo album

## 🐟 WHAT YOU DO 🐟

Each year after breakfast on the first day of school, take your children into the backyard for a photo shoot. Ask them to stand next to a favorite tree or bush, something that will allow you to see how tall they have grown since the previous year. Take their picture, and give them something from the garden such as a leaf or a small pod, to take with them to school the first day. Add the picture to a photo album containing the pictures from past years.

# Hearts on a Napkin

*I miss you more! —Anonymous*

When my children first attended preschool, they went for a half-day, 2 days a week, coming home for lunch. I was able to limit my teaching schedule to 2 days and 2 nights a week, and I was able to pick them up at noon every day. After they "graduated" to staying in school during the lunch hour, I wanted to connect with them during the longer school day and started this simple ritual.   —L. Nayer

## 🐟 WHAT YOU NEED 🐟

- A paper napkin
- A pen

## 🐟 WHAT YOU DO 🐟

When you pack your child's lunch, write a message on the paper napkin for your child. I used to draw a heart and write "I love you." If your child can't read, you can draw a picture of the two of you going to eat a muffin after school or going to a nearby playground. My children both remember their napkin messages and how it made their lunches seem more special.

# Young Child's First Performance

*Bright light*
*Star of night*
*Dance with joy.*
*—Louise Nayer*

Fear of public speaking has been said to be matched only by a fear of death. For children, performing recitals, dance concerts, plays, and the like can carry a similar weight.

We all have stories of the results of this fear. A boy named Johnny in my fourth-grade class urinated onstage, to his horror and the horror of 60 eyes staring at him. There are many other tales of upset stomachs, tears, even fainting. Sometimes, young girls in butterfly costumes dash to mommy or daddy when the lights dim.

How do we encourage our children to let their lights shine, have fun, and leave room for mistakes? If a 5-year-old does run to mom and dad and misses the performance, is that so terrible, so worthy of lectures and guilt? Also, how do we honor *all* the children who perform, while giving our own young person some special attention?   —L. Nayer

## 🐟 WHAT YOU NEED 🐟

- *Extra time with your child the night before*
- *Examples of people who performed and sometimes made mistakes, either from your own life or the lives of friends*

- A bouquet of flowers for every child (donated by all the parents)

## ❧ WHAT YOU DO ☙

First, make a commitment to attend the performance and include special others whom your child suggests. If your child is in grade school, don't dwell on or talk too much about the upcoming performance except to work out all the details.

The night before the big day, spend some extra time with your child. Relate a story about how you performed in a recital that may not have gone perfectly. Keep it light: "I forgot my comb, so my hair stood up on end" or "I missed a few lines and the stage was very quiet for a while, but we managed to finish the show."

Make it clear that you respect all the hard work your child has done to prepare for this performance. Try to connect with other parents through the teacher, and as a group contribute money for a small bouquet for each child, to be presented at the end of the performance.

Go out for pizza or ice cream with family and friends and offer a toast to your child for all the hard work, however the performance went.

# First Time at Sleep-Away Camp

*Mommy, I love you with two hearts. —YuWen*

When I was 9, my city school had a 1-week program for fourth graders to get us out in the country. I got strep throat 2 days before the bus left and was driven up later by my mother. I vividly remember the moment she left me and drove back to Manhattan.

When I was 10, I went to a church camp for 1 month. During the first week, I was so anxious that I stayed up until midnight, sitting in a big armchair in the common room. When the camp director made his rounds, he was surprised to see me completely awake.

Not every child has trouble with leaving home, but homesickness at camp is so common that most camps don't allow phone calls except in emergencies because they fear that children will fall apart when they hear their parents' voices. Many children are anxious, but most get over it and have a wonderful time making friends, playing in the great outdoors, and gradually learning to separate from their parents.

How do we make the transition to camp easier for a first-timer? Even if the child has friends or siblings going with him, getting on the bus to go far away can be a frightening experience.   —L. Nayer

## 🐟 WHAT YOU NEED 🐟

- *Photos of the family, including the family pets*
- *Flat stones*
- *A red marker*

## ➤ *WHAT YOU DO* ➤

At dinnertime a couple of days before the trip, bring out some photos of the family and the family pets that you will give to your child for the trip. You can put them in a small photo album that your child can look at on the bus ride and keep nearby in his cabin.

Go together to find special stones to represent you and your child, to be used as "touchstones." Use the marker to draw hearts on each stone. Give the stone you selected to represent yourself to your child and vice versa. One or both parents can do this.

Tell your child that while he is away he should hold your touchstone in his hand every night before he goes to sleep and remember that you are holding his stone and saying goodnight to him. "When you hold the stone, think of me and know that everyday I send my love to you as I hold my stone and kiss you goodnight."

# Teen's First Job

*Let me grow. Hold on. Let go. Let me free.*
*And please always see the good in me.*
*—Louise Nayer*

Most of us worked as teens, whether it was babysitting, mowing lawns, or serving ice cream at the local Dairy Queen. Perhaps the job didn't pay very much, but the act of getting to work on time, doing what was asked, and bringing home a paycheck is an important transition in the life of a teen and should be recognized.

Teenagers often get a bad rap, but there are many dedicated and responsible young people in the world. My daughters and friends of theirs clean up the beaches, go on AIDS marches, and sometimes contribute their allowances to good causes. They also get to work on time and do a good job. How do we honor them at a time when most of them don't want to be fussed over, especially by mom and dad? Here is a simple ritual that can earn them some extra money, a bit of an education, and respect. —L. Nayer

## ➤ WHAT YOU NEED ➤

- Your teen's favorite meal and sparkling cider
- A paycheck
- A Roth IRA application

## ➤ WHAT YOU DO ➤

At the end of the first pay period, cook your teen's favorite meal and offer a sparkling cider toast to a job well-done.

After dinner, present your child with an application form for a Roth IRA and agree to match her first paycheck with an equal amount of cash.

Show her the math: If she puts just $100 in the IRA at age 16, assuming 11 percent compounded interest, she will have $16,627 by age 65. If she makes $2,000 over the summer and puts her full summer's earnings into the IRA, she will have $332,549, tax-free, at age 65. If she likes math, she may want to do other projections. Explain to her that while money should not rule her life, it can make her life comfortable and allow her to help others as well.

Be a good role model for your teen. Show her how you save money each month, even if it's just the change in your wallet. Show her also how you use some of your money to help others.

# First-Time Driver

*It's not who's right. It's who's left.* —Anonymous

Children are the future, the hope of the world, the most precious beings to their parents. Yet in most countries, at 16 years old, young people get into powerful metal machines and begin adult lives on the road. It's a road sometimes terrifyingly nightmarish with speeders, drunken drivers, and road rage. Now, facing my own 15-year-old who will be getting a permit in San Francisco, I am aware of the need to trust her for the responsible person she is and of the need to create a ritual within our family to remind us all of the importance of this milestone in her life and that our hearts are always with her.    —L. Nayer

## ᕈ WHAT YOU NEED ᕈ

- Your teen's favorite dinner
- The successfully passed test from the Department of Motor Vehicles
- A contract between parents and teen
- A prayer for the road

## ᕈ WHAT YOU DO ᕈ

Make your child's favorite dinner the day she receives her drivers license. Ask her, ahead of time, to bring home the written driver's test as a memento and as something to refer to as she starts her driving career.

Write a contract with her, spelling out specific expectations of her use of the car. Make two copies of the contract and read it out loud to her at the end of the meal, with parents and child signing it and placing it somewhere safe.

## Sample Contract

Respecting the privilege of driving, I will:

- Wear a seatbelt and ask my passengers to do the same
- Drive at or under the posted speed limit
- Respect the rules of the road
- Drive with courtesy and caution
- Be home on time or call before I am late
- Take care of the car, reporting problems immediately
- Refuse to drink or use any drugs when driving

We will:

- Expect to be called if any problem with the car or passengers arises
- Come get you, no questions asked, when you need us
- Always take care of repairs needed on the car

Together, read out loud the prayer for the road or a special prayer you make up as a family. Place the prayer near where she picks up the car keys, and place one copy of the prayer in the glove compartment.

## Prayer for the Road

May you and your car and any passengers, day and night go
safely sober and alert
looking out for any who may endanger you
May you never rush
for your life is more precious

*than any missed appointment*
*May you always care for your car*
*for it takes precious cargo*
*May you always use good thinking*
*and know that you are always*
*in our hearts as you go*
*on your journeys*
*from place to place*
*May you always arrive*
*safely at your destination*

End the evening by telling your child how proud you are that she has successfully reached this milestone in her life.

# First-Generation College Graduate

*As we let our light shine, we unconsciously give other people permission to do the same.* —Nelson Mandela

I grew up with college-educated parents who expected that I finish college *and* graduate school, but the students I teach come from families where they are usually the first to finish college. They are the trailblazers.

Graduating from college is a big step for anyone, especially those who are first-generation grads. Most of my students at City College in San Francisco work 30 hours a week and take a full load of classes. Some also have family responsibilities. Pursuing a degree is a difficult road with few markers and sometimes not enough support. Too often, there is the temptation to quit school.

Many graduates are too busy with work and school to take much time out to acknowledge this significant step in their families' histories. They may even begin to feel disconnected from their families as they begin new lives.

Often, relatives cannot attend graduation because they live far away or the school issues limited invitations, so it is important to plan a special celebration to let the graduate know how this achievement honors the whole family.   —L. Nayer

## ❦ WHAT YOU NEED ❦

- College graduates
- A gathering of supportive family and friends

- The name of a special teacher who helped along the way
- A person to mentor

## ◖● WHAT YOU DO ●◗

One friend or relative should host a special dinner for the graduate and invite family members and friends who have helped the student along the way. Ask the graduate to name teachers who were especially important. Perhaps it was an elementary school teacher? Or a college professor?

If possible, invite the teachers to the gathering. Any teacher would be thrilled at the invitation. If a teacher lives far away, the graduate can write a letter with the good news. If the teacher is deceased, ask the graduate to speak about the teacher and why she should be remembered. Prepare a toast to the graduate, given by family members and friends expressing their pride in her accomplishments.

At the party, encourage the graduate to pick a person in the family to mentor, perhaps a young person who is having difficulties in school. If you are a first-generation college graduate, your breaking the mold may inspire other family members to pursue their dreams, even late in life.

# First-Time Voter

*Lift every voice and sing* —James Weldon Johnson

My grandmother was a suffragette in upstate New York, and my mother also worked for the rights of women in her work as a nurse and the editor of a nursing journal. They have both passed down to me a legacy of social action and the need to be informed and to have a voice through voting.

For years, my husband registered voters; I helped him, going door-to-door in San Francisco neighborhoods, encouraging people to go to the polls. There are many important measures to vote for, some in fine print, like voting to keep libraries open for longer hours, to fund neighborhood community centers, or to create small class sizes in elementary schools. The bills that get passed have profound effects on the lives of ordinary people. Here is a first-time practice to help a new voter begin a lifelong ritual of active participation in the community.   —L. Nayer

## WHAT YOU NEED

- A voter registration packet
- Family or friends
- A file folder marked "voting"
- The local newspaper for the day of your first vote

## WHAT YOU DO

A month before your first-time trip to the polls, go over your voter registration packet with family and friends. Discuss the issues, remembering that people have the freedom to express differing views on all issues.

Set up a night to study the issues over dinner at a local restaurant. Make this an annual gathering. Perhaps one of your parents or an uncle or aunt can go over your packet with you.

If you live in an area with district elections of representatives, call their offices directly and say, "I am a first-time voter. What are you doing for our district?" You may be surprised at the quick response.

After voting, set up a file with your first registration booklet and any letters you received from senators or representatives. You can also write down any referendum bills that you voted for that passed and had a positive effect on your life. Pass this file down to your children, nieces, nephews, or to a young person in your life who is going to the polls for the first time. Also, save the newspaper of the first day that you went to the polls. Your voting folder is a keepsake and a reminder to others that you took your vote seriously.

You are now a voting citizen and can make a pledge to yourself to continue to be informed, to vote, and to get others to do the same.

# First Apartment: A Moving-In Shower

*I get by with a little help from my friends.*
—John Lennon

When two people marry, all sorts of things happen to support their newly independent life together. There are showers, beautiful gifts, dinners, and shopping sprees. But when a single begins an independent life, usually nothing happens at all! Why is that? Today, many young men and women live a single life for many years. Some choose to stay single permanently and don't intend to marry. Though we may not consciously intend to marginalize singles, many wonderful people are unwittingly punished for their lifestyle choices in our couple-conscious culture.

This is a way for friends to celebrate an important milestone in the life of a close single, letting him know he is loved and supported.

## ⬤ WHAT YOU NEED ⬤

- A pen and paper
- A celebratory evening hosted by the friends
- Gifts for the apartment, both practical and beautiful
- Framed photos of close friends
- The verse "Friendship" by George Eliot in calligraphy, attractively framed

## ❧ WHAT YOU DO ❧

Make a list of useful items needed to set up housekeeping for the first time. These will include nonstick pots and pans, flatware, glassware, a toaster, a blender, everyday china, a shower curtain, flower pots—many of the same things couples need. Be sure to include items that are not only practical, but beautiful.

At a meeting arranged by a close friend, assign one well-organized person the task of coordinating a moving-in shower to be held just before or just after the guest of honor moves. The organizer should call to ask each shower guest to "register" for an item on the master list. Each person also should bring a framed photo of himself to the celebratory shower.

At the shower, ask each guest to present his gift and photo with a personal toast acknowledging this new step in his friend's life and offering his love and support. As each person finishes speaking, ask him to place his photo on a designated table, mantle, or wall. The framed copy of George Eliot's statement on friendship may be placed in the center, with the friends' photos around it as a "circle of friends."

Friendship is the comfort, the inexpressible comfort
of feeling safe with a person
having neither to weigh thoughts nor measure words
but pouring all right out as they are,
chaff and grain together, certain that a faithful
friendly hand will take and sift them, keep
what is worth keeping, and with a breath of comfort,
blow the rest away.
  —George Eliot

# RED-LETTER DAYS

*Certain days are cause for great celebration: going off to college, finding a job, getting married, having a child, retiring. These are moments to cherish, and the attention we give to them has lasting effects on our lives, helping us tuck away loving memories, reserves we can draw on during difficult times.*

*We honor ourselves and those around us when we take the time to mark these events, engraving on our hearts and minds the importance of what has happened on these days.*

# An Adoption Ceremony

*My heart knows you China girl of black night*
*in the red Changsha coals that warm your small feet.*
*It throws a rope wide across the brave clouds,*
*loops your dragon soul in soft cords of love.*
*—Virginia Lang*

When we brought YuWen home from China, we held a break-of-day ceremony on a rocky cliff overlooking the Pacific Ocean. She was dressed in red Chinese silk adorned with little gold bears and was surrounded by people close to our family.

Louise and "Godfather Jim" read beautiful pieces they had written, and our friend Claude read "The Song of Pure Happiness," a very old Chinese poem by Li Po. Another friend, Judy Kimmel, rang a Tibetan bell and one of my godchildren, Morgan Green, handed out red flowers for each person to present to YuWen.

Then, we all walked together down to the ocean and let the soft curling waves of the Pacific tickle her tiny feet. As we looked out over the ocean to her first home so far away, I was struck by how very different her life would be on this side of the ocean. I was very moved by this heartfelt dedication by the people who would now come to know and care for her as family.

Afterward, we shared a festive brunch given by our friends the Greens, and everyone got a chance to hold and play with YuWen, who was 10 months of age at this time.   —V. Lang

## 🐟 WHAT YOU NEED 🐟

- A special fabric or color from the child's birth country
- A setting in nature
- A small gathering of family and friends
- Selected readings, music, and flowers that reflect her heritage

## 🐟 WHAT YOU DO 🐟

If you sew or know someone who can, make a special dedication outfit in the spirit of the child's native country. For Chinese girls, the color red is the color of celebration. The flag of California, her new home, inspired the little golden bears on YuWen's gown.

Choose a setting in nature that has meaning for you. Ask close friends and family to attend a ceremony there and to bring something that is special to them—perhaps a bell, a flower, or a poem. Let each person read, sing, or play an instrument according to her abilities. The youngest in the group may want to offer to each person a flower native to the child's country of birth.

Join hands and say together, "Respecting the life and lineage of this child, we receive her gladly into this culture, this family, and these hearts. May the richness of her native culture be the seed that bears fruit in the fertile soil of our lives." Observe a minute of silence together. Then, celebrate with a meal that includes food from both cultures. In Chinese tradition, long noodles are eaten for long life.

Here is a poem I wrote to YuWen.

**For YuWen**

*A far wind blows*
*through your round flesh,*
*covers the oceans,*
*warms my long bones.*
*Your small heart beats*
*in the gold summer light,*
*in the long Yiyang shadows,*
*in the blaze of noon sun.*
*I need no compass*
*to find your boned hand,*
*no rod to divine*
*your soft parting lips.*
*We walk in locked step,*
*through the caverns of time,*
*through the mighty black ocean,*
*through the blue peacock sky.*

Here is a Native American adoption blessing.

*Friend, this day I take you in my arms and hug you*
*strongly.*
*And if it is meant to be,*
*Our Father the sun will, in his path over the world,*
*rise and reach his zenith,*
*Hold himself firmly and smile upon you and me*
*that our roads of life may be finished.*
*Here I touch you with my hand*
*and with the hands and hearts of the gods.*
*I pray to the wind of life,*
*That our roads of life may be finished together.*
*Friend, may the light of the gods meet you!*

Here is a beautiful blessing translated from the original Bengali by Rabindranath Tagore.

*Bless this little heart, this white soul*
*that has won the kiss of heaven for*
*our earth.*
*He loves the light of the sun, he loves the*
*sight of his mother's face.*
*He has not learned to despise the dust, and*
*to hanker after gold.*
*Clasp him to your heart and bless him.*
*He has come into this land of a hundred crossroads.*
*I know not how he chose you from the*
*crowd, came to your door, and grasped your*
*hand to ask his way.*
*He will follow you, laughing and talking,*
*and not a doubt in his heart.*
*Keep his trust, lead him straight and*
*bless him.*
*Lay your hand on his head, and pray that*
*though the waves underneath grow threatening,*
*yet the breath from above may come and*
*fill his sails and waft him to the haven of peace.*
*Forget him not in your hurry, let him come*
*to your heart and bless him.*

# Choosing a Spiritual Mentor

*Be ye lamps unto yourselves, be your own confidence.*
*Hold to the truth within yourselves as to the*
*only lamp.* —Buddhist saying

When my daughters, Sarah and Laura, were 8 and 6, Ginny, Dean, and Heather's home was a special haven to them. Ginny and Dean cooked many elegant dinners for special occasions, and at a young age, the girls were allowed to handle crystal glasses filled with sparkling apple cider.

Ginny's family also came to the children's soccer games and piano and dance recitals, and had parties that included my parents, then in their eighties. It was certainly a merging of two families and of all the generations. It was only natural that Ginny and Dean would become Sarah and Laura's godparents.

Many families pick godparents for their children through a church christening-and-naming ceremony, bringing their children into their religious tradition. We attended the Unitarian Church, but there was no formal godparent ritual, so we created our own. This ritual can be for families not involved with a place of worship or for godparents who were present at a church ceremony but want to rededicate themselves to their godchildren, making a commitment to now older children that they will continually be involved in their lives. —L. Nayer

## ➤ WHAT YOU NEED ➤

- Godparents, a godchild, and the godchild's family
- Readings written or selected by both families
- A special dinner
- Formal clothes for the event
- Special gifts to give the children as keepsakes

## ➤ WHAT YOU DO ➤

Choose an evening for the ceremony and prepare by writing or finding selected readings. The meal can be shared, each family cooking one or two dishes. It adds importance to the evening if everyone dresses in his finest and sets the table elegantly.

After the meal and before dessert, begin the readings. Let each person read a favorite poem or passage or say something heartfelt. In our ceremony, my husband, Jim, read a passage from the Bible about the importance of adults giving their best to children. I read a poem from poet Kenneth Patchen; Sarah, at 8, recited a poem about how happy she was to have a godfamily! Laura, at 6, watched wide-eyed and entered into the discussion when she wanted.

After the readings, Ginny, Dean, and Heather got up and made a commitment to Sarah and Laura. The commitment is written by the godparents as a reminder of the deep promise to hold the children in their hearts and minds and to help guide them as they grow into fully developed human beings. You may choose to use the one we used:

"We promise to love and guide you without judgment, to listen to your deepest feelings, and to help you find your purpose in life. We will always be there as extra shoulders to lean on when times are tough. Call on us. We embrace all of you, everything you feel, everything you think, and everything you will become."

Ginny got each of the girls a magic wand, in the spirit of the fairy godmother. She said that every time they rub the wand, they will be calling on her love for them. Any kind of special object can be passed to the children: a book, a painting, a necklace, or something from nature like a stone or a shell.

After the readings, serve cake and spend the evening doing what the families like to do best. Our families sang and played piano into the evening.

# Honoring Special People in the Lives of Families

*With love, all turmoil ceased. —Gabriela Mistral*

There is always enough love to go around. Many of us have people we remember from our pasts who were not relatives, adults who visited and gave us special attention, played blocks with us upstairs—not commenting on our messy rooms—read us stories, taught us how to French braid our hair, and sometimes babysat when our parents went out.

In our family, "Uncle" Bill taught Sarah and Laura to be artists, spending countless hours drawing with them. He also taught them how to garden. One dear friend decorates sugar cookies with them each year for Christmas. With her environmental expertise, she also takes us all on hikes, recently introducing the kids to the tidepools by Año Nuevo State Reserve in Pescadero, California.

Families are often quite insular, protective, and sometimes jealous of outside influences, but when a trusted close friend enters a family, wonderful exchanges can and do happen. The children receive more love, and the parents get needed breaks from the demands of family life.

How do we make these special people feel honored for all that they do for the children and for the whole family? And how can families remember how important they are to the lives of special friends? Here is one way to honor these friends and welcome them into the family.   —L. Nayer

## 🐟 WHAT YOU NEED 🐟

- The friend and family together
- The friend's favorite foods
- A photo album with pictures taken over time
- A handmade card

## 🐟 WHAT YOU DO 🐟

Invite your friend over for her favorite dinner, prepared by the whole family. You can make it special by dressing up and setting the table as you might for a holiday. On the handmade card, ask everyone to write something about why the friend is important to them: "I love the paint set you bought me and love to draw with you" or "I love the walks we take at Point Reyes National Seashore and will remember the dappled horses we saw along the way." Give your friend the gift of the photo album, including photos of the family with her. Promise to keep filling it as you create more memories. Give the card and afterward offer a toast: "You are family!"

# Coming of Age:
# A Father-and-Son
# Pilgrimage

*I am on my way running,*
*I am on my way running,*
*Looking toward me is the edge of the world,*
*I am trying to reach it,*
*The edge of the world does not look far away,*
*To that I am on my way running.*
*—Anonymous*

When my friend Peter Borenstein was a young man, his father, Mark, took him to the gravesite of Peter's great-grandfather in Poland. Most of the family was killed in the Second World War, so it was a particularly moving pilgrimage for father and son.

I was struck by how deeply Mark felt about making this trip with Peter and how rich it was for Peter to see not only his place in the Borenstein family, but his place in the history of the world. The forging of identity is so critical in the development of children, yet many of us have no rite of passage for a child that invites him to take his place and to see that place as important. —V. Lang

## ❧ WHAT YOU NEED ❧

- A father and son
- Pictures, letters, and memorabilia from the past

## ➤ WHAT YOU DO ➤

Choose a day such as the anniversary of a grandparent's death to begin to talk to your son about his family history. Take out pictures and letters and, if possible, invite elders over to recount stories from the past.

Over a vacation, take a trip to the birthplace of his grandparents or to the cemetery where they are buried, where you may make a rubbing of the tombstone together. Help your child to see those who came before him as real people whose characters and personalities are parts of him.

At a special shared meal, give him something that was special to grandfather, like a favorite book, a special woodworking tool, a certificate of baptism, or a pocket watch. This gift is a symbol of trust in him. With it, include a letter letting him know how you feel about him and sharing your hopes for his future. Let him know he honors the family in all he does, but he is free to be himself and to reach beyond the limits of the past as well.

# Going Off to College

*Watch well over your seed children!*
*Speak wisely to these our new children!*
*They will be your first speakers and the*
*peacemaking shields of your people.*
—Zuni tribe

When my friend Kathy Martin sent her son, Jeff, off to Columbia University in New York City, she put him on the plane, went home, and cleaned his room for hours, just sobbing and sobbing. After so much anticipation during his senior year, she was exhausted and had not had time to take in the feelings of this important transition in her and Jeff's lives.

When a child leaves home, there is such a mix of feelings—sadness that a chapter is closing, joy that the child has succeeded in reaching an important milestone, fear of the child's future without parents standing by, hope that what has been taught will serve to support the child in his independent life. If we have done well, our "seed children" will indeed become "the peacemaking shields" honoring all of us with their intelligent choices and strong bodies.   —V. Lang

## ✒ WHAT YOU NEED ✒

- *A gathering of close friends and family*
- *A celebratory meal*
- *A camera*
- *Personal letters*

## ⬤ *WHAT YOU DO* ⬤

Invite close friends and family to a send-off dinner at the child's home. After dinner, gather in a circle and light a candle to be passed around. Ask each person to take the candle in hand and speak from his heart words of blessing, congratulations, loss, whatever he is feeling. Then, offer a toast such as this one: "We trust you to make good choices, to honor your body, to engage your mind, to follow your dream. Go forward in love and light, knowing we hold you in our hearts with every step you take."

Take pictures of each person at the dinner. Later, take the photos and frame them in a composite frame or cut and paste them into a collage of all the people who love him. You may want to add personal sentiments under each picture or a group wish like "We love you and trust you. We are with you in spirit every day of your life." This will remind the new student of all the love and support that go with him to his new dormitory room.

If photos are a challenge, ask each person to bring to the gathering a personal letter to the student to be put in a scrapbook for the student to read during the often lonely first year away from home. *Life's Little Instruction Book* started out as a father's words to his son as the young man set out in life. Take the time to make your letter your heart's best effort.

# The Interview: Finding Your Strength

*She carries all creatures in her soul.*
*She is a hawk, a fly, a cat, a minotaur.*
—For Laura, *Louise Nayer*

After having had a series of rats, parakeets, and goldfish because I didn't think my allergies could withstand a furry beast, we got our dog a year ago. I've been amazed, as has my husband, at how much our dog adds to all of our lives, allowing us to shower our affection on a fuzzy being, who responds in kind.

Penny, our nonallergenic bichon frise, also gives us strength. When the children feel sad, they hug her to them and she licks their faces. When we are happy, we throw her ball down our long hallway and watch her endless puppy energy.

Animals can help people's lives in all sorts of ways—even imaginary animals! When I went on an interview for my tenure-track job at City College of San Francisco, my good friend Jeri suggested I imagine a lion going with me.    —L. Nayer

## 🐟 WHAT YOU NEED 🐟

- A scheduled interview
- A good imagination

## 🐟 WHAT YOU DO 🐟

As much as a week before your interview, imagine that you have a lion by your side, giving you strength and courage. Close your eyes and see its full hair and long mane.

On the day of the interview, make sure you continue to keep your lion with you, even if you are called into the "hot room" quickly (as I was) or the room is crowded with people and the lion has no room to lie down. I placed him by my feet, under the table, with his head up, alert and completely ready to give me the strength I needed. Other friends who have gone for interviews have also conjured up an image of the lion and presented themselves with great strength to their prospective employers.

# The Wedding Tree

*Our roots are with each other, now,*
*in the veins of the tree, in the glistening earth.*
—Louise Nayer

When my stepdaughter, Bonnie, and George got married, they followed an old Quaker tradition and planted a tree in their backyard to symbolize their marriage and how it would grow over time.

The wedding was a flurry of activity, with people flying in from all over the country, many relatives from both sides, friends, and a party at their house the night before the marriage, with music and dancing. One of the most tranquil moments for Bonnie and George was when the tree was planted in the backyard, with a few people watching this small ceremony.

Bonnie says that, to this day, whatever else is going on in her life, she always remembers to water the tree and often looks at it, watching it grow, knowing that it symbolizes her marriage to George. Family and friends who know of the tree and were there when it was planted also have a special feeling for it, even if they live far away from Bonnie and George's backyard, as we do. —L. Nayer

## ❦ WHAT YOU NEED ❦

- *A tree to plant that will last many years and is right in terms of weather conditions for where you live*
- *A shovel*

## ➤ WHAT YOU DO ➤

If you are leaving for your honeymoon immediately after the wedding, choose a time before the wedding when you can both be present to plant the tree. You can dig together or you can ask for help in digging the hole. My husband, Jim, helped Bonnie and George. Gather a few special people around to watch the tree planting.

When the tree is placed in the ground, you may choose to say a few words like these: "We promise to water and care for this tree everyday and in all types of weather, as we will care for each other."

Let there be a few minutes of silence in the Quaker tradition. If you live in an apartment, you may purchase an indoor tree, such as a bonsai. Or, find a public or private place that allows tree planting and perform your ceremony there.

# A Wedding Anniversary

*Hereafter, in a better world than this,*
*I shall desire more love and knowledge of you.*
*—William Shakespeare*

I've always thought a wedding anniversary should amount to more than a dinner out. As each year of married life passes, one should get the opportunity to renew the contract or at least renegotiate the terms. No job description stays the same, so why should the job description for husband or wife? It takes great communication and self-respect to keep a marriage alive over the years. Sometimes, we forget that both individuals must thrive for the marriage to survive.   —V. Lang

## 🐟 WHAT YOU NEED 🐟

- Two evenings before your anniversary
- The willingness to be direct

## 🐟 WHAT YOU DO 🐟

Two nights before your anniversary, write letters to each other focusing only on the good things that have happened to you in the past year of marriage. Exchange letters and allow yourself to feel whatever is there; if it was a difficult year, you may simply want to express gratitude for the support of your spouse during this time. Celebrate this in some fashion, with a dinner out or a good bottle of wine.

The next night, write letters asking for help to improve

something about your life together. Do you need more help with the children? Would you like to spend more time with friends? Is money a constant worry? Exchange letters again and discuss your feelings. There may not be easy solutions, but bringing your deepest feelings to light is essential if you are to deepen your commitment to one another. Write in the first person: "I would like more time to paint."

On the anniversary itself, exchange gifts personally selected for each other (no toasters, please). Give careful thought beforehand to what would mean the most to the other person, and forgo items you need for the house. Consider "adventure gifts" you may never have purchased before, like a hike at sunrise with a Thermos of coffee, a Swedish massage for two, a poetry reading in which you offer one perfect rose, a handwritten poem, or a promise of a date night once a week.

Make your gift as personal and intimate as possible. One of the most beautiful poems I know, a romantic seventeenth-century piece, is an excellent gift for a woman who enjoys a long and mature marriage to give to her husband. I include it here for any woman lucky enough to feel this way.

## To My Dear and Loving Husband

If ever two were one, then surely we.
If ever man were lov'd by wife, then thee;
If ever wife was happy in a man,
Compare with me ye women if you can.
I prize thy love more than whole Mines of gold,
Or all the riches that the East doth hold.
My love is such that Rivers cannot quench,
Nor ought but love from thee, give recompence.
Thy love is such I can no way repay,

*The heavens reward thee manifold I pray.*
*Then while we live, in love let's so persever,*
*That when we live no more, we may live ever.*
—Anne Bradstreet

Here is a short but moving poem for a lover to offer.

## Old Song

*Take off your clothes, love,*
*And come to me.*
*Soon will the sun be breaking*
*Over yon sea.*
*And all of our hairs be white, love,*
*For aught we do.*
*And all of our nights be one, love,*
*For all we knew.*
—Robert Creeley

# The Card Shower: A Birthday Tribute

*No spring, nor summer beauty hath such grace,*
*As I have seen in one autumnal face.*
—John Donne

It is sad to admit that our culture associates aging with loss. Beyond the younger years, birthdays are often greeted with crude jokes about crow's-feet, hair loss, and other declining capacities. We are focused more on what we cannot do instead of on what we have become.

When we see the beautiful autumnal face of a woman whose life has been richly lived, we know there is much to celebrate and acknowledge on the day of her birth. Here is a ritual intended to honor an older woman for all she brings to the lives of those who love her. It works for men too.

## ☙ WHAT YOU NEED ❧

- A blank journal
- A person to act as coordinator
- A pen

## ☙ WHAT YOU DO ❧

If the elder is fortunate to live near most of her friends and family, buy a blank journal and paste a recent photo of the honoree on its cover. With the help of an organized family coordinator, circulate the journal among the honoree's dear friends and family members.

Ask each person to write about a quality that she appreciates in the honoree. For example, "Grandfather, you are my model of honesty and compassion. Happy Birthday!" You may wish to recall a treasured memory: "You are the most patient grandmother who has ever lived; I would have failed algebra without you!" The sentiments need not be long, just heartfelt and personal. Present the book as a group on the birthday. It is sure to be a most treasured gift.

When Louise's godmother turned 80, she took part in a "card shower" coordinated by her godmother's daughter. Each person wrote a heartfelt sentiment on a blank card and sent it to the daughter, who created a master scrapbook of all the cards. If distance is a challenge, this is a good option.

# The Autograph Book:
# A Retirement Keepsake

*Yours till Niagara falls. —Anonymous*

Recently, I came across a wonderful bit of memorabilia—my Aunt Katherine's autograph book. In her time, autograph books were precious keepsakes that gathered quotes, rhymes, and good wishes of trusted friends and family over a period of time.

Her book includes entries from 1917 through 1940, tracing her life from the First World War to her distinguished career as one of the first operating room nurses in the country during the early years of anesthesia. My favorite entry is a John Ruskin quote written to her by Sister Anna Ebert of Lankenau Hospital in Wynnewood, Pennsylvania: "When love and skill work together, expect a masterpiece."

As I read the carefully considered words of so many people who had loved and respected my aunt, I thought about how wonderful it would be to create such a keepsake today as a retirement gift for a special person whose work or character is noteworthy and who remembers this elegant, old-fashioned custom.   —V. Lang

## ➤ WHAT YOU NEED ➤

- *A good-quality autograph book*
- *The names and addresses of colleagues and close friends of the elder*
- *A response form*
- *Three to 6 months' time*

# 🐟 WHAT YOU DO 🐟

First, buy an attractive, hard-covered gift book, ideally one of the old-fashioned ones that were small and distinctive. If you can't find one like this, there are many small scrapbook or journal-style books available in stationery stores.

Find a way to get the Christmas card list, Rolodex, or address book of the person to be honored. Write to the key people (you may need help from the honoree or another relative), and enclose a simple return form and a self-addressed, stamped return envelope.

On the form, draw a box sized to fit the pages of the autograph book. Ask each person to handwrite in ink a short but very personal message to the honoree, in the space given (entries of two to six lines; rhymes are great!) and to sign it and return it to you as quickly as possible. Give the deadline as 1 month before the date you wish to present the book. When you have received the entries, cut out the boxes and paste them into the book to be presented at retirement as a gift from colleagues.

# Honoring a Mentor

*We are all in the gutter, but some of us are looking at the stars.* —Oscar Wilde

I have a true stargazer friend. In the midst of a divorce, she planted a magnificent garden, tending with the dedication of a monk her weeping cherry, apricot tulips, and the tender grasses that grew between rocks. She would go out at midnight with a special lamp on an extension cord to garden under the night sky.

When Dean and I married, Judy brought lemons she had grown that were still attached to the stem. These lemons and Louise's wedding poem were my most memorable wedding gifts.

Some time later, when I grew *my* first lemon, I took it to Judy in a spirit of triumph. I am no gardener. She was just as pleased with the significance of that first lemon as I was.

We all have someone who has taught us something special about life, someone who has offered us a new view of our possibilities and ourselves. This is a ritual to honor such a person.   —V. Lang

## ☙ WHAT YOU NEED ❧

- *Someone you respect who has taught you something*
- *An item such as a plant, tree, quilt, or poem that symbolizes the lesson learned*

## ◆● WHAT YOU DO ●◆

Some day when you have done something well, think about how you learned to do it. Whether you have grown an especially beautiful lemon, baked brownies beyond description, produced your first children's play, or climbed a mountain, someone has inspired you—someone who would love to know of your success. Plan a visit to your mentor and take along a symbol of your accomplishment. The greatest gift you can give a teacher is understanding the lesson!

# The Accomplishment Book

*Things won are done;*
*joy's soul lies in the doing.*
—William Shakespeare

An art student winning a contest, a developmentally disabled child in the Special Olympics, and a Rhodes Scholar receive awards. Sometimes, awards are given for participation in an event because not everyone can win. Awards elicit pride and self-esteem. One girl may get trophies for winning soccer games and another for a beautiful butterfly collection.

Richard DeFoe, who works at my husband's senior citizens' center, is developmentally disabled and has built his whole life around the Special Olympics. He has won many trophies for track. The awards he has received add immeasurable joy to his life.

Accomplishments never end, whether they are visiting a sick friend, volunteering for a church committee, or taking a niece out to lunch. Expanding the definition of accomplishment will help everyone view the world differently.

Many awards get lost when people move. Here is a way to keep the memory of accomplishments in a book that can become a keepsake.   —L. Nayer

## 🐟 WHAT YOU NEED 🐟

- A large scrapbook
- A camera

## 🐟 WHAT YOU DO 🐟

When your child wins an award certificate, date one page of the scrapbook and put it there right away. If your child does something special in the house (like paint a room), photograph her doing the activity and place the photo in the book. Fill the book with records of accomplishments for each year, making sure to expand your view of an accomplishment to include not only a good report card or a trophy but things as simple as a child making dinner for the family for the first time.

This book will be a prized possession for her to look over and will help her to see how much she has done when she is feeling down. It also will help a child to know that you appreciate not only what society expects of her but also the special way she expresses her love and personality around the house.

You can also keep an accomplishment book for an older adult who might think, "I don't do anything anymore."

# TRANSITIONS

We are always in transition. Nothing ever has the tidy beginning or end we like to imagine. The minute we think we have captured something, it is no longer ours; the chrysalis becomes the butterfly, the fire turns to ash.

Somewhere along the way, we have learned to dread transition and change. But it doesn't have to be that way. When we can see the transitional state as an ideal situation—in which we are free to exceed prior limits and assumptions—our lives can be enriched beyond our wildest expectations. Transition times offer us the chance to learn flexibility and grace, like the willow bending in the wind.

# The Life Collage: Envisioning Change

*If you want to sing out, sing out*
*And if you want to be free, be free*
*There's a million ways to be*
*You know that there are.*
—Cat Stevens

Many of us see life as a collage, a kaleidoscope of images. Where do we fit in the picture? Where are we going? In collage workshops, participants create pictures of their desires through images and words focusing on what they want in different areas of their lives: love, travel, money.

In her book *Creative Visualization*, Shakti Gawain shows how mentally picturing what you desire can allow it to appear in your life. Creating a collage is a concrete and creative way of envisioning a reality that you may be stepping into at any moment. The successes of this type of envisioning have been myriad. Some examples are a friend of mine who found the exact apartment she pictured in San Francisco and an older woman who had been single for many years but found a mate within 6 months of creating her collage.

Perhaps the consciousness raising that goes with this exercise can allow dreams to come true. Along with becoming aware of what you wish for, let the childhood thrill of cutting and pasting yield to adventures you may never have imagined.   —L. Nayer

## ◗ WHAT YOU NEED ◖

- An assortment of magazines such as nature, women's, sports, and art magazines
- Sturdy paper or poster board
- Scissors and glue sticks
- Pens
- Other objects if you wish, such as buttons, ribbons, or shells

## ◗ WHAT YOU DO ◖

Plan collage time. Gather together as many magazines as you can that contain a variety of images and words. Before you start, focus on your desires. A new home? More money? A mate? More travel? More time alone?

You can divide the collage into different areas—money in one area, where you might paste your salary goals for next year; another corner can show two people lovingly holding hands across a table; another corner can display images of traveling on a ship to Alaska.

You can also cut out words, prayers, poems, or messages, or write your own words in between the pictures. Always put a picture of yourself in the collage. Many people place themselves in the middle of the collage, the images surrounding them.

If you are not sure of a focus, cut out images that appeal to you and see what kind of life picture emerges. For a more 3-D effect, paste the buttons, ribbons, or shells onto the collage. Be as varied as you wish.

Display the collage prominently in your home so you and others who love you can see what you envision. Who knows, it may also qualify as an objet d'art.

# Saying Goodbye: When a Friend Moves Away

*For me who go,*
*for you who stay—*
*two autumns.*
—*Taniguchi Buson*

When I was growing up, we moved five times as the Ford Motor Company transferred my father from plant to plant. Each time, I had to say goodbye to friends, knowing I would probably never see them again.

This was sad and confusing for me and left me with the belief that people you come to love go away. Now, many years later, I can see how painful it was for my brother and parents, too, and how much our family needed ways to make these transitions more gracefully. Here is one simple way to weave a happy memory with a loved family that is being left behind.    —V. Lang

## 🐟 WHAT YOU NEED 🐟

- *Colored ribbons at least 1 inch wide*
- *An indelible marker*
- *Cardboard*

## 🐟 WHAT YOU DO 🐟

*Ask each member of the family that is moving to recall a happy memory that was shared with the family staying behind* and write it on a ribbon. For example, "I will always remember the Christmas when Anna thought Santa got stuck in the chimney." Ask the other family to do the same.

Weave the remembrance ribbons together like a lattice pie crust, using the cardboard as a backing, and present them to the departing family at a farewell dinner. If you like, make two weavings so each family can have one.

Hang the weaving where all family members can see it and be reminded that friendship does not end with distance. Remember to call and write often, especially in the first year away.

# Making Choices

*Life does not give itself to one who tries to keep all its advantages at once. I have often thought morality may perhaps consist solely in the courage of making a choice.* —Léon Blum

Recently, my younger daughter, an avid soccer player, decided to switch from a highly competitive team to a recreational team. Even though she is 11 years old, the month building up to the change and the day of the decision were not easy. We all had many feelings about the situation, but in the end it was her decision and we let her make it. I began to think of how she could best let go of the old team and adjust to the new one without losing her self-esteem and enthusiasm for soccer.

Changes in a child's life, such as changing schools, teams, or households, can be very difficult. It is important to acknowledge the child's feelings and to help her work through painful memories rather than suppress them.   —L. Nayer

## ➣ WHAT YOU NEED ➣

- Your child's favorite cake with icing and two candles
- The parents or family members and friends most important to the child

## ➣ WHAT YOU DO ➣

After a family dinner, give the child some time to talk about the change in her life. Perhaps there is more she wants to say, even though the decision has already been made. Maybe she feels that someone wronged her or she feels that she has to give up some precious friendships. Let her talk until she is finished, ending with her hopes for the new team, school, and so on.

Ask your child to light two candles, close together. As she lights the first candle, let her say, "I'm leaving my old team and, though I may miss some friends, I know that I have made the right choice for me. I wish the team all the best, as I wish myself all the best!"

Next, ask your child to light the second candle and say, "I move to my new team, with the love of my family and friends. I trust myself completely and I made a good decision!" Then, ask your child to blow out both candles and serve the cake to the guests. Change can be delicious!

# Welcoming a Young Woman into the Circle

*You bring me back where old women dress me in satin*
*let me sing with lips of red wind.*
—Louise Nayer

My sister, Anne, lives in the Virgin Islands and talks about a special spot at Hull Bay, a sand crescent between two green points jutting into the Atlantic Ocean. Rocky coral reefs visible as dark blotches mark the otherwise breathtakingly turquoise sea dotted with fishing boats.

One night, under a full moon, a group of women met at Hull Bay to honor a 12-year-old they had known for many years, celebrating her transition from a girl to a young woman. Though most of us don't live in paradise, full moons exist all over the world. Here is a ritual to help a young woman feel proud of growing into womanhood and connected to a community of women she can turn to during the pivotal years of adolescence.   —L. Nayer

## 🐟 WHAT YOU NEED 🐟

- *A group of women gathered under a full moon*
- *A young woman who has recently reached puberty*
- *A small gift from nature*
- *A leather pouch or small purse*
- *Food and drink brought by everyone*

## 🐟 WHAT YOU DO 🐟

Form a circle around the young woman and ask each person to speak to her, recounting memories from when she was an infant to the young woman she is now. Each woman can also speak of this transition into womanhood in her own life, as a way of supporting her through this change.

Next, have each woman speak of her hopes for the young person and walk to the middle of the circle to give her a hug and present her with a small gift from nature, such as a piece of coral or a seashell that can be put into the small pouch and kept in a special place.

When the ceremony is over, eat and drink something together. If you are fortunate enough to live in the Virgin Islands, you can then swim in warm waters under the full moon! End the evening with a blessing:

> We wish you courage to stand up for yourself,
> intelligence to make good choices,
> strength to pursue your goals
> and more than enough love surrounding you
> as you go on this new journey and adventure.
> Call on us at any time.

# Walking Sticks:
# A Father-and-Son
# Journey

*Thou shalt shew me the path of life;*
*in thy presence is the fullness of joy.*
—Psalm 16:11

My friend Jeri noticed something as her son became a teenager—
the balance of power and ability shifts between father and son.
Suddenly, the son may run faster than his dad or be better able
to reach up to a high cabinet or throw a ball farther.

When a son turns 13, a dad who likes camping can take
his son on an expedition, setting this time aside to teach his
son some of the skills he has learned over the years, passing the
torch of manhood and creating a special time between the two
of them.   —L. Nayer

## ● WHAT YOU NEED ●

- *Camping gear, including a compass and water purification system*
- *A campsite with fire ring*
- *Two walking sticks found in nature*
- *Carving tools*
- *A present from dad to son*

## ● WHAT YOU DO ●

*You and your son should plan the trip together, but you*
*choose the trail and camping site. The young man must complete*

a list of essentials for the adventure—from the amount of drinking water needed to the renting of a bear-proof container (if you're in bear country!) to a list of food and other necessities.

Before or during the trip, show your son how to use the compass and water purification system, survival skills that are now to be passed down. The first evening away, when night falls, share the building of a simple pyramid-style fire, letting the younger man start the fire as a symbol of his growing manhood.

The next day, on a hike, each of you can choose a walking stick from the brush. That evening, carve your sticks with your initials and other images that are significant to you.

As you carve your sticks, discuss what has been important to you throughout your life and given you strength. Then, point out the strengths you see in your son, giving him confidence that his father believes in him as he enters the teen years.

You may then choose to give your son something passed down from previous generations, such as an arm patch, a medal, or a pocketknife.

When you return home, leave your walking sticks near the front door as a symbol of your commitment to spend time together and to continue to talk about what is important to you.

# The Letter Shower
# for a Teen

*Ask the questions now; then someday quietly, without*
*noticing it you will live some distant day into the*
*answer.* —Letters to a Young Poet *by Rainer Maria Rilke*

The teenage years are ones of transition from child to adult. Have you ever seen a young adult holding on to a favorite stuffed animal while waiting to go to a rock concert? The night before Sarah started high school, she crawled into bed with me for a few minutes. We both knew what was going on and just held each other.

Through the Unitarian Church, Sarah was in a coming-of-age ceremony, but we wanted to do something at home, too, and came up with the idea of a book of letters from those who love her as well as a work of art that she could treasure.

I found some artwork representative of the teenage transition time—three different circles of images: a butterfly in the middle, dragons in the next circle, and in the last circle, angels. Sarah was moving from being a little girl into a larger world, transforming like the butterfly and protected by the angels.
—L. Nayer

## ➽ WHAT YOU NEED ➾

- Letters from relatives and adult friends of your child
- A scrapbook with a decorative and personalized
  cover

- Important pictures that represent different stages in your child's life
- A work of art that speaks to the age of 13

## 🐟 WHAT YOU DO 🐟

Contact relatives and friends to ask them to write a letter to your child when she turns 13. Tell them that the letter needs to be sent by a particular date. Some suggestions might be to write to the child about her strengths, her courage, her talents, and how they trust that she will become a wonderful adult. Remember the special moments of childhood and offer words of wisdom, without preaching.

Sarah's dad wrote in part of his letter, "I see you not only as a beautiful, intelligent, talented, and strong young woman, but as a soulful traveler on this Earth, a daughter I deeply love." Later, he wrote, "Find the path that is truly your own." Whatever you write, write from the heart.

Collect the letters in a scrapbook, interspersing them with the pictures representing important points in your child's life. Have a special dinner and invite a few of the important people in your child's life. Light candles, bring out a cake, and present the book. Bring a positive light to the newfound freedom and independence that your child is experiencing.

Along with the book, find a painting that best expresses the transitional nature of the teenage years. Give her the painting as well. She will most likely want to hang it up in her room. If that is not the case, let her choose where she wants to display it.

# Laying Aside a Child's Love Object

*A banana left*
*at night*
*on a plane*
*Since then*
*he's been stuck*
*in the sky*
*and we call him moon.*
—Jesus Carlos Soto Morfin

I have a terrible memory of losing my childhood blanket. The day my mother decided I should be done with it, she told me she was just going to wash it, but it never came back from the wash. Anyone who thinks this is no big deal to a child is dead wrong. I can still remember every detail about that exchange and the look on her face that said something really big was going down!

So when YuWen's beloved stuffed-toy camel got left on an airplane, I was devastated. How could I ever explain that "Jim" was gone? I made up an elaborate story about how he had stayed on the plane because it was going on to Paris and he wanted to see the Eiffel Tower. When her godfather went to Europe, he sent her a postcard from Jim and a drawing of the camel sitting in a café near the Eiffel Tower—wearing a French beret and looking at a framed picture of YuWen that he had taken along!   —V. Lang

## 🐟 WHAT YOU NEED 🐟

- Keen observation of your child
- A special moment to celebrate "Jim"

## 🐟 WHAT YOU DO 🐟

Once your child has outgrown her need to have her "Jim" as a daily appendage, take a moment together to preserve him so that she can see the importance you are giving him. Ask her what she thinks he would like. She may wish to place him in a satin-lined bed or in a shadow box that can be hung, or she may be happy simply making a special place for him on a bedroom shelf.

Let her say words from her heart to him as you give "Jim" a place of honor. Fortunately, YuWen found a new love after Jim, a bear named Albert that she wraps in a carefully chosen tea towel when it rains. What happens to Albert matters to her . . . and *I* still want my blanket back!

# Locks of Love:
# A Celebratory Haircut

*Fair tresses man's imperial race ensnare,*
*And beauty draws us with a single hair.*
*—Alexander Pope*

What is it about hair? In the Bible, Samson is tamed when Delilah cuts his hair. In Eastern philosophy, the hair on our heads lies on the crown chakra, the energy center that connects us to the larger community and the cosmos. In Western religions, you often see pictures of angels with halos in roughly the same place as the crown chakra. Perhaps that is why cutting it has so much power for us and carries such symbolic meaning.

In Peru, I had the opportunity to cut the hair of a young girl named Brigida—the group with which I was traveling participated in her coming-of-age ceremony at the base of one of the most sacred mountains in Peru, Ausangate Knot. Each of us was asked to cut a small piece of Brigida's hair from the nape of her neck and place it in a ceremonial bowl. As each of us took the scissors, we called her by name and gently stroked her head. Those of us who spoke Spanish whispered words of love and support.

Afterward, we shared a celebratory meal of potatoes and roasted guinea pig and gave small gifts of money to Brigida. I will always remember the look on her face as we crossed into her world, her time, and her Andean home through this simple ritual. While ritual haircutting is not observed in our culture, it may be meaningful as part of a coming-of-age ceremony for a young girl who has made the decision to cut off long hair. —V. Lang

## ☞ WHAT YOU NEED ☜

- A child who has made the decision to cut off long hair
- Family and special friends
- A decorative bowl
- Scissors
- A hairdresser
- The address of Locks of Love

## ☞ WHAT YOU DO ☜

Sit in a circle and place a beautiful bowl in its center. Beginning with parents and grandparents, ask each member present to stand, take the scissors, and cut a small piece of hair from the nape of the child's neck, calling the child by name and speaking a private message of love and support in her ear.

Place each lock of hair in the bowl in the center of the circle. Pass the scissors from person to person until each person has had a turn. When the circle is complete, join hands and spend a few minutes in silence together. You may want to give small gifts of money or attractive hair ornaments for the child's new look.

Ask your hairdresser to join you, or make an appointment for her to cut the hair professionally in the salon later that day. Make a gift of the clipped hair to Locks of Love, an organization that makes wigs for children with cancer. Be sure to contact them for detailed instructions before you cut. You may reach them at Locks of Love, 1640 South Congress Avenue #104, Palm Springs, FL 33461.

# Keeping Faith with a Newly Disabled Friend

*I thank God for my handicaps, for through them,*
*I have found myself, my work, and my God.*
*—Helen Keller*

I learned recently of a men's group that meets every week at the home of a newly handicapped man whose name is Joe. When Joe became paralyzed, he started to fall into a deep depression. With a wife and young children, his despair was beginning to have severe consequences for his family.

The men's group began to gather once a week at his home to go out for a lunch date. Joe is always asked to choose whom he wants to ride with to lunch. Joe's spirits have markedly improved because of this weekly ritual.

When I heard the story of Joe, I realized that for no real reason I have been holding back from meeting my new neighbor who is bedridden. Her husband and son, who care for her, told me that most of her friends have fallen away since her illness. Even her sister doesn't come around. Why is it so hard to look suffering in the eye?

A Chinese expression advises, "To have a friend is to love the crows on his roof." When misfortune comes to people we love, we need to learn to love their crows.   —V. Lang

## ✧ WHAT YOU NEED ✧

- *2 to 3 hours once a week*
- *A housebound or handicapped friend*

## 🐟 WHAT YOU DO 🐟

Organize a group of friends to plan a weekly group event that your handicapped friend can enjoy. Think about preparing your car for his comfort and making certain the restaurant, movie theater, or home you choose to visit is one that is accessible and easy to navigate.

If the person is bedridden, take a picnic to his room each week with real napkins and fresh flowers. Take a book he would enjoy, and take turns reading out loud and discussing it as a book club. Or become a writing group, sharing feelings through words. The beginning of my writing life began in a writing group of four that met in Louise's bedroom once a week. That group grew to eight and is still meeting 8 years later.

# From Couple to Parents: Creating Space for a New Love

*Today we are three; what happened to you and me?*
—*Virginia Lang*

One of the greatest challenges for a couple who decides to have a child is making the transition from lovers and friends to lovers and parents. The presence of a newborn begins a profound shift in the relationship as the husband finds his way toward a new understanding of himself as father, and the wife, as mother.

While there is delight and awe in the process of redefinition, there is also loss of place. For a while at least, the parents' new roles can seem like bit parts in the high drama of the newborn who now takes center stage. Conscious recognition of this fundamental shift from couple to family may help to ease this transition.

## 🐟 WHAT YOU NEED 🐟

- *A quiet time to be together as a couple, close to the time of birth*
- *Two pencils and paper*

## 🐟 WHAT YOU DO 🐟

*Express to each other your hopes for your future as a family. You may wish to write down your thoughts and then* offer them to each other, one person at a time, or you may choose to write a statement of hope as a couple, like the one that follows.

## A Statement of Our Hopes as New Parents

As our marriage blossoms with the new life entrusted to us, we hope:

To respect and deepen the love that brought us together

To fall in love with our child, while we keep our love alive

To make time for each other, to listen, to play, to just be

To move into our new roles as parents with humor and acceptance

To support each other with understanding and compassion

To acknowledge the loss of freedom with largeness of spirit

To draw on the support of family and friends, while finding our own way to parent

Type up and frame your statement of hope and place it where you can be reminded of it!

# Coming in Second: Losing an Opportunity

*Men are always sincere. They change sincerities,*
*that's all. —Tristan Bernard*

Some time ago, my husband was a hair's breadth from a dream job—the one he never imagined would materialize. After five trips and more than 20 interviews, the job was offered to someone else. Unfortunately, there was no consolation prize.

After a few weeks of intense anger followed by deep sadness, he began to see that he had learned something from the experience that he would apply to the next opportunity. Together, we talked it through over and over, realizing that this kind of loss also needs a process to allow the anger and frustration to subside and new possibilities to emerge.   —V. Lang

## 🐟 WHAT YOU NEED 🐟

- A time and place to be alone with your most trusted friend, spouse, or mentor
- Two hours
- A pad and pencil

## 🐟 WHAT YOU DO 🐟

Seat yourselves comfortably in a place you will not be disturbed. Make sure no phones or faxes will interfere, and give yourselves 2 hours, minimum, for this two-part ritual.

## Part I

Ask your friend, spouse, or mentor to use the pad and pencil to take notes while you speak freely, allowing any and all feelings to emerge unedited and uncensored! The friend can ask these or similar questions:

1. What went wrong?
2. Was it avoidable?
3. Did you get a poor reference? Can you talk to that person?
4. Was there a stronger candidate; do you feel you screwed up?
5. Are you left feeling unfinished because you never really found out what happened?
6. Is there any gracious high road left to take? A letter expressing future interest, a thank-you for the opportunity to interview?
7. Was there an injustice that would warrant legal action?
8. Was the process too long? Unfair? Too demeaning?
9. Was the job misrepresented?
10. Are you well-suited for this work, job, or process? Do you want another shot?

When you have exhausted these thoughts, take a break and walk around a bit to clear your head.

## Part II

Return to your places. With your friend continuing to write down key words, brainstorm all the things that were good about the opportunity. No matter how silly, just blurt things out, like "I would've gotten an office with a window!" or "The promotional possibilities were unlimited." Go on until you have identified all the things you wanted from the position and will want from the next one.

When you feel really finished, have the friend read the list of comments back to you. Then, using the list of what you just said, make a statement out loud, like this one: "I intend to find an even better position that offers me promotional possibilities, terrific colleagues, generous benefits..." and so on. Fill in the blanks with the wish list. Give a stated date by which you'd like to find this position. In 3 months? By next spring?

Express thanks for any lessons learned from the experience and be sure to thank your friend for her thoughtful listening. Close the door softly on this episode, keeping in mind that burning bridges may not be in your best interest. The same company or even opportunity may come up again for you. Let hope begin to replace the anger, and ask your unconscious to go to work on attracting an even better opportunity to you.

# Home Sweet Home: Creating the Home You Want

*Come here. Sit beside your childhood.*
*Drink from the old words.*
*You will find your own clock.*
*Listen, it's your heart.*
*—Louise Nayer*

In our twenties, thirties, and sometimes later, many of us drift between relationships, jobs, and places to live. All too often, we wake up from this constant drifting to realize we are not "home."

At the age of 24, after finishing graduate school in Buffalo, I packed all my belongings in a 1968 Camaro and drove across country, alone, maps on the passenger seat. I called my parents from a phone booth in the middle of Colorado while watching the hawks circle the sky and chickens run in circles in a nearby yard. I was trying hard to be free of the past. Years later, I wanted the opposite—to create a home.    —L. Nayer

## WHAT YOU NEED

- *The desire to create a home of your choice*
- *Two pieces of paper*
- *Pens or pencil*

## WHAT YOU DO

On the first sheet of paper, write the word *home* in the middle of the page and draw a circle around it. Coming out of the circle like tentacles, write down any words you associate with your childhood home. Some words that come to mind might reflect where you lived, the noise, the people, difficulties, joys, sorrows. For example, you might use words such as *noisy, music, alcohol, brother, moving.* Under each of those words, you can write more about the noise, the music, and so on. You will most likely have a wide range of memories from early childhood to high school. If writing this brings up too many bad feelings, make sure to have a good friend or counselor to work with you.

On the second sheet of paper, a day or two later, make another circle with tentacles and write down what you would like in your new home. What would be different? Was your childhood house noisy and would you like more silence? Was your childhood home lonely and would you like a lot of people at the dinner table? Write down whatever comes to mind, again using as much detail as possible.

Put away your first "map" and place your new "home" on the refrigerator. Look at it often, reminding yourself of what it is that you want.

# City Walks:
# A Nighttime
# Adventure for Men

*Boys came bearing cornstalk violins*
*And they rubbed the cornstalk bows with resins*
*And the three sat there scraping of their joy.*
*—Galway Kinnel*

A few years before my husband turned 50, he began to take night walks in the city with his good friend Brad and a few other men. The city walks symbolized a desire to take to the streets. At midnight when they climbed above the cover of descending fog on Twin Peaks, they always encountered the ever-changing view of San Francisco at night.

The group scaled San Francisco hills from Mount Davidson to Twin Peaks, sometimes climbing for 3 hours, coming home exhausted and exhilarated. They explored the city as they had as young boys with skinned knees and stories to tell.   —L. Nayer

## 🐟 WHAT YOU NEED 🐟

- A friend or two to walk with you
- Water and snacks
- A flashlight
- Maps of the city
- A first-aid kit
- Reflectors on your clothing

- A knapsack
- A cellular phone (just in case)

##  WHAT YOU DO

Plan your city adventure with your friends, deciding how far the group can realistically walk and agreeing to push a little past each one's comfort zone. Take food and drink, a flashlight, and other necessities. Make safety a priority.

Have fun just being together on an adventure, the type you remember from childhood treasure hunts and days of just going out in the woods to play. Let all money and family cares drift away for the evening as you enjoy time with your buddies.

If there is time when the hike is over, go out for a drink and recount stories of the adventure. My husband and his friends have had many stories to tell—discovering blackberry brambles near the University of California Medical Center, getting poison oak, and calling the fire department to rescue a cat trapped in a sewer. Each adventure was new and exciting.

# Embracing Change: A Woman's Midlife Journey

*In a dream you are never 80. —Anne Sexton*

The minute we hang on to something, it begins to change. Love changes, children change, our work changes, our bodies change. In this culture, we often resist change, anesthetizing ourselves with shopping or food, alcohol or drugs, escapes of a thousand natures, anything to numb the feeling that the ground is shifting under our feet, to keep the illusion of control.

Lately, my menopausal body has been knocking me about, trying to get my attention. I haven't wanted to listen, to admit that a profound change is occurring and that I am becoming a different person in many ways. I have come to see that the energy expended in resisting this transition would be far better directed toward self-acceptance and humor, if I am to grow older gracefully and happily.  —V. Lang

## ❧ WHAT YOU NEED ❧

- *Time alone once a week for as long as it takes*
- *A journal*
- *A Litany of Acceptance*
- *A recent photo of yourself*

## ❧ WHAT YOU DO ❧

As you begin to notice your changing body, spend some time alone every week with a journal. Write about your body, your mind, the changes you are experiencing, and how you feel about them. Compose a personal litany of self-acceptance or use the words of this one:

## A Litany of Acceptance

It is time to please myself.

It is time to treat the life-giving powers of my body with gentleness.

It is time to allow the creative power within me to find new expression.

It is time to open my heart in self-acceptance so I may love and serve others and myself with all I have learned.

It is time to step into the middle of my life grateful for the wisdom, grace, and courage I now possess.

During this time, take a thoughtful look at yourself. Frame a recent picture of yourself and place it where you can appreciate what you look like now. You may want to adopt some of the following new practices.

- Consider a change of image. Buy clothes with simpler lines and of better quality. If you wear perfume, find a new, more complex scent. Maybe you'd like to grow your hair impractically long or change your look in some other way that expresses who you are now. If you have trouble doing this alone, plan a "menopause makeover" in a spa or retreat setting where you can create a treasured memory with a few close women friends over fine aged wine.

- Try new physical activity. Perhaps you would enjoy yoga or swimming more than jogging. If you don't like exercise, at least plan to take a good walk each day.

- If you are tired of cooking, try eating out or preparing simpler meals instead of cooking so often. Simplify daily tasks that rob you of creative time: clean less, paint or write more.
- Organize a small women's group for support and friendship. Learn to meditate as a group, and enjoy the peace and respite of your own good company.
- Find a younger woman to mentor either in her career or personal life.
- If you are a camper or would like a more rugged rite of passage, consider the Vision Quest, a solo wilderness experience to get in touch with yourself and help redefine your goals. For information, contact Peregrinations, 8 White Oak Court, Menlo Park, CA 94025.

# Losing a Job

*If we had no winter, the spring would not be so*
*pleasant: if we did not sometimes taste of adversity,*
*prosperity would not be so welcome. —Anne Bradstreet*

The workplace today often consists of huge mergers, corporate downsizings, and profound displacements. Many hard-working people who have been loyal to their employers have found that loyalty means little when a company is sold to a conglomerate. In academia, scholars who have counted on tenure have not been prepared for the financial hardships many colleges and universities have weathered. Manual laborers without technical skills are sidelined in the new information economy.

As the sweeping ebbs and flows of global economics wash over us, it is easy to feel powerless and abandoned. This is the very time when friends, family, and ritual matter most.

## 🐟 WHAT YOU NEED 🐟

- *Close friends and family members*
- *A circle of chairs*

## 🐟 WHAT YOU DO 🐟

*Gather together trusted friends and family members who have an appreciation of what you are going through. Choose only those who will be not be judgmental (no voices of, "I told you so").*

*Arrange a circle of chairs or of pillows, if you prefer. When everyone has been seated, the person who lost the job* should speak first, thanking the group for their support and relating the facts of the lost job.

Each person should then ask whatever questions she may have and offer whatever help is appropriate. A parent may offer temporary financial help, a best friend may offer child care during the job search, someone else may have a contact or even another job to offer.

Each member should call the unemployed person weekly until he finds another job, offering moral and practical support for as long as the search takes.

# When the Rings Come Off: The End of a Marriage

*I never hated a man enough to give him diamonds back. —Zsa Zsa Gabor*

No single moment embraces the dissolution of a couple quite like the day when the rings come off. You want to *do* something with the rings, but what?

## 🐟 WHAT YOU NEED 🐟

- *The ring*

## 🐟 WHAT YOU DO 🐟

We asked a bunch of people what they did to mark the moment the rings came off and how they dealt with it afterward. Here are the best ideas. Feel free to choose one or come up with your own based on any of these.

- "My mom crafted her rings into a gold pendant in a jewelry-making class. She cut the rings, flattened them, rounded the pieces, and placed them side-by-side in an offset vertical design. To finish the pendant, she had a goldsmith professionally set the diamond into the design. The people at the class cheered her on, yelling, 'Go, Elizabeth!' as she cut the rings. It was definitely a powerful moment in her life. I imagine her tiny 5-foot-1-inch frame at some sort of power saw, with massive goggles on and sparks flying!"

- "I returned my ring to my husband with a letter that explained how I felt about the 28 years we'd had together and what I hoped to achieve without him."

- "I knew someone who had it melted down, with other jewelry her ex gave her, into a nugget that she wears on her charm bracelet. The act of melting it down was closure for her."

- "I threw mine in a cup with old screws and other odds and ends in the kitchen junk drawer. Once every 2 years or so, I'm looking for something and find it. That's the moment of ceremony. It's the tiny epiphany—more of a reminder—that I've moved on successfully."

- "I have a friend whose parents split when she was a teenager. Her mom gave her wedding ring to her and her engagement ring to her sister as keepsakes. It meant a lot to my friend because it was a way for her to hold on to the times when her parents were happily married."

# Passing the Torch: Honoring a Special Elder

*A teacher affects eternity; he can never tell where his influence stops.* —Henry Brooks Adams

A few weeks before my Uncle Bush died, we gathered at our family farm where he had spent many happy hours. Mowing the meadow was always his special love, and he spent hundreds of hours on the tractor in communion with the land. After mowing, he would go in the house, take off his yellow straw hat, and ask my mom for a big glass of ice tea.

At this last gathering, he brought his work shoes, as he had so many times before. Though he hasn't mowed in a decade, he still came ready to work, at 91 years of age. All afternoon as he and I sat and watched my husband and brother mow, he kept turning to me and commenting, "They really like it, don't they?" I knew then that he had what he needed to let go of this life, the sight of the next generation caring happily for his beloved farm.

I felt so glad that he had had this final satisfaction and could leave his life having passed the torch. He died peacefully in his sleep 5 weeks later.   —V. Lang

## 🐟 WHAT YOU NEED 🐟

- *An elder member of the family*
- *Special time together*

## ⬥ *WHAT YOU DO* ⬥

Invite the elder to watch a younger member of the family perform something the elder loved to do—perhaps a grandson can cook an old family recipe, a daughter can tune up the car, a niece can sew or knit.

If there is a specific task the elder performed for the family but can no longer manage, such as carving the turkey on Thanksgiving, ask him to teach his technique to a younger member; or if he has already done so, let him watch his student perform. Though the task or skill may be as simple as mowing grass, it may hold great significance for him.

# Saying Goodbye to a Home

*Barn's burnt down—*
*now I can see the moon.*
*—Masahide*

When my Aunt Margaret and Uncle Albert sold their home, I think I was more upset than they were. This simple red brick home was the place of many happy family gatherings, a place I always felt safe and deeply loved.

I knew it was time for Aunt Margaret and Uncle Albert to simplify, yet all I could think about was how I would miss the crunch of their green metal rockers, the smell of their boxwoods, the burgundy-and-turquoise kitchen where many hands had made light labor of washing dishes after a holiday meal. I have never before nor since had so much feeling for a house. It was hard to say goodbye.   —V. Lang

## WHAT YOU NEED

- A day in the house before the packing begins
- A camera
- A candle

## WHAT YOU DO

While things are still in place, photograph every room, capturing the placement of beloved objects and special collections. Be sure to photograph "Uncle Albert" in his favorite chair or "Aunt Margaret" where she always sat at the table. Make copies of the prints and keep the photos in two small acid-free albums, one for you and one to give later as a gift.

During the packing, offer to help sort and sift through the memories so you can share one more very special memory in the home.

As you leave the house for the last time, take a moment to walk through each room with a small candle in hand and say goodbye to each room. If the family is together, join hands and say, "We are grateful to have shared so many happy moments here."

# Retirement: Beginning a New Journey

*Age is an opportunity no less*
*Than youth itself, though in*
*another dress.*
*And as the evening twilight*
*fades away*
*The sky is filled with stars invisible by day.*
—Henry Wadsworth Longfellow

Some people work until their last breaths, dedicated to their jobs or unable to retire because of finances. For many people, though, retirement offers new opportunities—time to paint or draw again, time to go fly-fishing, more time with family.

Many people have identified themselves with their jobs so much that they find little pleasure in other activities, mainly because they have had little time or mental space to explore other venues. Those who have avocations, passions for something, do better during retirement.

My husband is director of a senior citizens' center and has seen many people blossom in their later years, becoming painters and sculptors, finding and sometimes reclaiming talents from their childhoods. How do we make the transition smoothly? There is no easy answer, for retirement has to do with health, finances, relationships, and mental attitude. But this ritual may help people find a new path in life.   —L. Nayer

## 🐟 WHAT YOU NEED 🐟

- Twelve index cards and a pen
- A bowl
- Time alone once a month
- A calendar

## 🐟 WHAT YOU DO 🐟

A year before you retire, write down on each index card one avocation that interests you: constructing remote control boats, drawing, going to gem shows, playing golf, singing in a choir, whatever moves you. On the back of each card, write down the name of one month of the year. Place all the index cards in a bowl.

If your card for January says "constructing remote control boats," spend some time during that month researching the field, buying magazines related to model boats, visiting hobby shops, and connecting with others who enjoy the same activity.

Make sure to write down the avocations on your kitchen calendar, one for each month of the year. By the time you retire, you will have some idea of which world (or worlds) you wish to enter as a retiree. The preparation will be invaluable. You can leave the world of work certain that many other people will welcome you with open arms.

# Leaving Home:
# Helping an Elder Move
# to Assisted Living

*I want to come home to my overstuffed chair, to the
smell of baking chocolate, to the purple of lilacs. My
heart keeps time by my grandfather clock. Can you
hear it now? —Margaret Bauer*

When my Aunt Margaret moved from her home to assisted
living, she found the transition difficult. Though people in her
new home are kind and the place is attractive, the loss of
freedom is very unsettling to her. Meals are prepared, beds
made, prescriptions delivered all without any input from her.
She has come to feel she is simply not needed in her own life.

To make matters worse, during the move she had been too
ill to oversee the placement of her possessions. Often, when I
visit, she asks me where her rocking chair has gone or "Will
Johnny get the grandfather clock?" Moving to a hotel-like atmosphere has robbed her of her sense of identity and control.
Her objects, though not important in themselves, have now
taken on symbolic importance for her.    —V. Lang

## ☞ WHAT YOU NEED ☜

- *A camera*
- *Special items such as favorite furniture, special jewelry,
  and tableware*
- *A small photo album*

- *A pen*
- *Handmade items from children, artwork, trophies, and special cards*

## ☙ WHAT YOU DO ❧

Photograph all the best-loved furniture and special items that will not accompany the person into assisted living. Place them in a special photo album and write under each picture where that item has gone. If possible, photograph each item in its new location with the grandchild, son, daughter, or friend who is now enjoying it. You might choose to put a large-type caption underneath each picture with a thank-you quote from each recipient.

When you visit your elder loved on at the assisted-living home, make it a point to talk about how much the item is appreciated and make it a ritual to look at the album together, remembering happy times in the past. Let the children present their handiwork to the elder.

# The Seven Generations: Envisioning the Future

*I plan for it, when I plan for it, it nicely drops into*
*position just as I wish.*
*Earth's support I first lean into position.*
*As I plan for long-life happiness,*
*it yields to my wish as it nicely drops into position.*
—*Navajo chant prayer song*

What is your great-great-great-granddaughter doing right now? Where does she live? In an overpopulated city? On another planet? What is she wearing? Chinese silk, a detox uniform, a space suit? What does she eat? Food? Nutrient powder? What is she like? Cloned? Genetically perfect?

Do these questions sound like science fiction? Have you thought about life in the third millennium, and if not, why do you think you haven't?

Native American families looked out seven generations in their thinking and decision making. They thought about how their actions in the present would affect the next seven generations in the future. In our rush to get what we think is rightfully ours, we seldom act as if there will be any future generations at all.

We consume and discard with abandon, unwilling to look at our dying planet and the sicknesses of mind and body that are endemic to our consuming mindset. How would we live if we *really* cared about future generations and thought about their well-being?

## 🐟 WHAT YOU NEED 🐟

- A weekend alone with your spouse once a year
- A pencil and paper
- A tape recorder

## 🐟 WHAT YOU DO 🐟

Picture your great-great-great-granddaughter and -grandson in a third-millennium lifestyle. Consider what they will need that may no longer be available on the Earth. Think about what you are doing today that may be undermining their future.

Decide how you want to use the resources and time available to you now. This may mean anything from limiting your family size to using and advocating solar energy to working for an effective recycling program in your community to creating a new educational model for your children. Start by addressing questions like these:

- What do we know about the world's population, and how does that relate to our plans for the size of our family?
- What do we know about efforts in our community to safeguard precious wildlife, wetlands, or beaches? How can we help?
- What are our children learning that will equip them for the pace of technological change? Are they creative enough for the next century? Are they getting what they need from our school system?
- What are we buying that is destructive to the Earth? Are we supporting companies whose values we respect? How do we treat animals and other species that have no voice?

● Where do our investment dollars go? Do we know enough about the industries we support? The charities we support?

Make two lists, one of short-term strategies like recycling or eating more organic food, the second of plans with more far-reaching consequences, like limiting family size. Tape-record your commitments. Play it on the same day the next year to gauge your success, and update your family's commitment as you learn more.

Some ecologists think it is already too late to save the Earth. But we can still prove them wrong. Vow to inform yourself and to bring consciousness, compassion, and seven-generation thinking to every new decision your family makes. We're running out of time.

# LOSS

To live a full life is to experience many small deaths, to often tumble out of the comfortable nest of our expectations, to learn about grief. When we find the courage to meet life head on, the loss of a family member, loss of a friend, loss of health, or loss of youth can all be our teachers, the ways we learn the meaning of compassion.

The pain of loss forces us to think, to discover, and to seek out others, drawing them to us in new and intimate ways. Loss is an entryway to new understandings, an invitation to explore the rain-soaked, rutted roads of our lives, and an admonition to cherish times of comfort and joy.

# How to Bury a Goldfish

*Even in the smallest things, we express who we are.*
—Virginia Lang

If you have a child who has lost a pet, you know how difficult it is to talk about death. Did you say too much? Did you say too little? When YuWen was 2, she lost a goldfish because her well-intentioned mother overfed it.

As I contemplated the usual trip to the toilet, I thought about what a horrible message I was sending. This precious thing that had contained life and had meant so much to her was about to get the same treatment as her digested dinner! I chose instead a simple backyard burial, with a role for YuWen to play.   —V. Lang

## 🐟 WHAT YOU NEED 🐟

- *The dead fish*
- *A gardening glove*
- *A small plot of ground*
- *A trowel or a shovel*
- *A flower*
- *A calendar and pen*

## 🐟 WHAT YOU DO 🐟

*Ask your child to see for herself that her fish is no longer breathing and has no further need for her care. If it feels right, have her gently hold the fish in her hand (using the glove, if you prefer) and carry it outside to a small plot in the garden or near a tree. Then, dig a small hole and let her place the fish in it.*

Hold hands with your child and say with her, "We will miss you and we're glad you came to live with us." Then, gently cover the fish with soil. YuWen likes to sing, so she made up a song for the fish.

Finally, place a flower on the spot and visit the site once or twice in the next week or so. If you like, you may want to place a small marker made by the child or a special stone on the site. Circle the date of the death on the calendar to indicate its importance.

For a beloved family pet like a dog or cat, you may wish to wrap the animal in a soft cloth and choose a designated animal burial space in your yard, or have the animal cremated and scatter the ashes in a place that is special to the family, like a lake or a flower garden.

# Remembering a Loved Pet

*A four-legged friend, a four-legged friend,*
*He'll never let you down.*
*—Roy Rogers, about his horse, Trigger*

I recently got a letter from my friend Aldona thanking me for writing to her when her beloved dog, Penelope, died. She said she saved the letter and tucked it away in a memory box that contains Penelope's leash, bandanas, and Halloween pink tutu!

When Penelope died, Aldona and her family displayed flowers from friends, cards, and photos—including the album of photos they had developed over the years—on an "altar" on the dining room table. Having a ritual place to grieve really helped the whole family and honored the memory of a true family member.   —V. Lang

## 🐟 WHAT YOU NEED 🐟

- *A place to gather memorabilia*
- *Items that belonged to your pet, such as a leash, bed, special toys*

## 🐟 WHAT YOU DO 🐟

*Develop a family "altar" in memory of your pet on the dining room table or on a mantle. Ask each member of the family to add items to the altar like small flowers or handwritten notes. Keep cards, flowers, and photos of the pet on your altar* for as long as it seems right. You may want to frame a particularly good photograph of the pet and mark it with the date she became part of your family and the date she died.

Sometimes, friends don't understand all the fuss over an animal. Discuss this perspective on animals with your children so they can convey your family philosophy.

> For the animal shall not be measured by man. In a world older and more complete than ours, they move finished and complete with extensions of the senses that we have lost, or never attained, living by voices we shall never hear. They are not brethren, they are not underlings: they are other nations, caught with ourselves in the net of life and time, fellow prisoners of the splendor and travail of the Earth.
> —Henry Beston

# The Keepsake Shelf: When a Young Child Loses a Parent

*When I get to the farm, I open every drawer;*
*I look in the breakfront where she kept the linens,*
*Under the yellowed tablecloth with the slate gray roses,*
*In the whatnot drawer in the funnels and sieves,*
*In the button box, in the memories of smocked dresses,*
*In the highboy under blankets with torn bunting,*
*In the smell of her hankies worn soft with tears.*
*Where are you mother? Where have you gone?*
*—Virginia Lang*

When a parent dies while a child is still young, that death reverberates through the rest of the child's life. Some parents who know they are terminally ill are able to prepare their children a bit by gathering together objects that can be kept as cherished mementos, helping parent and children begin to deal with this enormous loss. The keepsake shelf can be anywhere in a child's room or in the closet if the child wants to keep the place a private area.

## ● WHAT YOU NEED ●

- *A tape recorder*
- *A journal book*
- *Photos*

- Cherished objects or clothing
- Perfume or scents

## 🐟 WHAT YOU DO 🐟

If it's possible for the parent to speak into a tape recorder, ask him to speak from the heart and give the child confidence that he will grow up to be a strong person who has been deeply loved and will continued to be loved. This very private tape can be placed on the keepsake shelf and listened to as needed.

Ask the parent to write as much as he can into a journal book, lovingly communicating with his child. Ask other adults to find photos of both parent and child in happy times together. Collect the parent's special objects, such as a favorite mug, album, or book, to be kept on the shelf.

Place on this special shelf a bottle of perfume or a scented piece of clothing that reminds the child of the parent's smell. Let the child know that it is normal and perfectly okay to want to be reminded of the smells surrounding the one who loved him so much. Make it clear that the keepsake shelf is personal and that no one may touch it without the child's permission.

# Losing an Unborn Child

*We are all unformed like the universe with its black
holes, its explosions, and its brilliant illuminations.
That some of us leave before being born just means
that they reach the stars earlier. Look up, their lights
shine on us. They have become stars, perfectly
symmetrical, pointing the way. —Louise Nayer*

Losing an unborn child is profoundly saddening. The physical exhaustion and the emotional feeling of loss may persist for months and even years. Many women are afraid to talk about their feelings. Typical responses are often inadvertently insensitive: "You're young, so you have nothing to worry about; you can always have another one;" "Children can be so difficult; enjoy your freedom."

A woman thinks of her unborn child on the anniversary of the due date. How old would the child be? What talents and characteristics would the child have? Here is a ritual that may help a woman who has lost a child before birth to begin to accept and integrate the loss in her life.

## ●➤ WHAT YOU NEED ◆●

- *Friends (or one close friend)*
- *Healing hands*
- *Beautiful music*
- *Refreshments*
- *A pen and paper*
- *A tree*

# 🐟 WHAT YOU DO 🐟

Pick a date. It can be significant (the anniversary of the loss or the due date). Have the woman lie down on a couch or bed, and ask her friends to gently lay their hands on her so she is completely relaxed. Play soothing music. Let the woman express whatever she wants to about this particular event in her life—tears, anger, nostalgia, or even the simple joy that her friends are there to acknowledge a part of her that she's kept private.

Then, share a cup of something hot and go into a room for writing. Designate a speaker to say, "You are holding your baby in your arms. Feel your strength as a mother, how secure you make your child feel. Now, you are singing a song to your baby, your beautiful voice gently rocking your baby to sleep. Feel the love you hold in your heart and your hands, a love without beginning or end."

Then, ask the mother to speak: "I'm sorry I will not hold you in my arms, but I will always hold you in my heart." Ask the mother to name the baby if it's comfortable for her to do so. Let her say the name out loud. Ask her to close her eyes and hold the baby in her mind's eye. Tell her to call up this moment of love and support anytime she wants.

Sometime later within the year, go as a group to plant a tree in honor of the child. If the mother has no yard, you might donate a tree to a public park, a city street, or a special place you like to visit.

# Accepting Infertility: When Life Isn't Fair

*I am a slice of myself,*
*a bloody red gash*
*in the center of the moon.*
*—Virginia Lang*

Many women who want children suffer deeply when they cannot become pregnant. Some choose to pursue an often long and exhausting road of infertility treatment; others allow nature to take its course. Because I lived through this deep disappointment, I know that no amount of support or words of comfort could begin to address my deep feelings of loss until some of my anger was released.   —V. Lang

## 🐟 WHAT YOU NEED 🐟

- Time alone in nature
- The poem "The Song of the Barren Orange Tree"
- A branch
- A journal and pen
- A litany of healing

## 🐟 WHAT YOU DO 🐟

Find a quiet place in nature to be alone. Read silently "The Song of the Barren Orange Tree."

### Song of the Barren Orange Tree

*Woodcutter.*
*Cut my shadow from me.*

Free me from the torment
of seeing myself without fruit.
Why was I born among mirrors?
The day walks in circles around me,
and the night copies me
in all its stars.
I want to live without seeing myself.
And I will dream that ants
and thistleburrs are my
leaves and my birds.
Woodcutter.
Cut my shadow from me.
Free me from the torment
of seeing myself without fruit.
—Federico García Lorca

Allow yourself to feel all the sadness and rage that is building within you. Scream as loud as you like for as long as you like. If it helps, find a branch and break it into many pieces, hitting it as hard on the ground as you can.

When you are exhausted, let yourself cry hard for as long as you wish. Later that night, write out your feelings in a journal. Before you go to sleep, say silently or aloud a simple litany like this one:

I am whole.
I am well.
I accept myself fully, just as I am.
My nurturing heart is whole and fertile.
I will allow a new self to emerge.
Life is not fair.
This is not fair.
I will go on.

"The Place in My Soul" is a piece I wrote to express some of my feelings. I include it here to help you get started with your own reflections.

## The Place in My Soul

> I need to find the place in my soul where I can simply rest.
> Hug my knees to my breaking heart and rock myself to death.
> I need to find the well in my soul where I can draw out
>     these fears,
> Feel sorry for myself as long as I want and drown in an
>     ocean of tears.
> I need to find the fire in my soul that will burn away this
>     grief,
> Leave it in ashes at the foot of my bed and sweep it to release.
> I need to find the wind in my soul that will blow in life
>     and hope,
> But until that day will come, I ask for courage just to cope.

# Deepening into Grief:
# A Ritual for Loss

*In a real dark night of the soul it is always 3 o'clock in the morning.* —F. Scott Fitzgerald

There are times in life when all we want to do is cry. When my mother died suddenly, I was so shocked and sad, I remember wandering into Grace Cathedral in San Francisco and just sitting and sobbing. A priest walked up to me and sat down, his arm over my shoulder, and asked, "What's wrong, little tiger?"

The tiger is my animal and I have often been likened to one, so it took me aback when this man, who didn't know me at all, saw through my tears to the stronger person within. He talked with me for a long time about the loss of his wife and his deep sadness when she died. Then, he scribbled his address on a piece of paper and asked me to let him know how I was doing, someday. This chance episode was one of the dearest moments in that long, dark time.

Friends often feel they have to cheer you up in sad times, but I think that grief has a lot to teach us and that getting on with our lives can begin only once the deep sadness is dealt with physically. Here is a way to let your body own and allow deep feelings of grief.   —V. Lang

## ✒ WHAT YOU NEED ✒

- One hour each day
- *The Age of Grief* by C. S. Lewis

## 🐟 WHAT YOU DO 🐟

For 1 hour each day, for as many days as it feels necessary, take the time to be completely alone. Sit or lie down comfortably and let whatever you feel rise up into your body from feet to head. Try to allow your body to completely feel your grief, no matter how bad it gets.

Take deep, cleansing breaths whenever you need to, and stay in your experience as best you can. Give your mind something to do. Ask yourself, "What is the sensation I am feeling? Where does it hurt? How hot am I getting? How fast am I breathing?" If it helps, draw or write to express what you feel, holding nothing back.

During this period of grieving, avoid distractions, tedious people, shopping, drinking, and all other diversions that take you away from your feelings. It takes some time and some courage to grieve, but we are built to take it and we can survive deep grief and grow from it, if we honor ourselves and go slowly, one day at a time. It is important to remember that others are grieving too. This is an excellent time to let the words of others who have grieved speak to you. Read C. S. Lewis's *The Age of Grief* and poems like this one.

### A Wail Sighting off Kehoe Beach

The great heavy glass of the ocean
that falls to its knees in obeisance
to the land, then is yanked back home
in foam by the ankles, cannot
contain my grief.
Each black wave like loam curled back by the plough,
fritters its top away in lace as its power
tips and dives, yet I plunge more deeply.

*Stink of the sea's detritus—the boas*
*of sea kelp decay; the crabs*
*like books of sodden cardboard matches dried—*
*all covered with busy flies—are not more sorry than I.*
*Blue ocean–blue sky.*
*Timpani of wave thunder, and snare*
*of pebbles and expended waves, and the sigh*
*of the last before the silent silk wipes*
*a mirror in the sand and leaves,*
*—let me cry.*

—James McColley Eilers

# The Death of a Parent: An Intimate Goodbye

*A man's dying is more the survivors' affair than his own. —Thomas Mann*

Before the father of my dear friend Sharon Swinyard died, he had started to play his violin again. One day, driving home from the doctor, he turned to Sharon and said, "I'm old now, aren't I?"

Active until the age of 92, he had never stopped to think about his age until that moment. When he died, his daughter decided to let him lie in his bed while she gathered her sister, her mother, and her closest friends around his deathbed. We lit candles, arranged a vase of stargazer lilies, and kept a vigil for hours, recalling memories of him as they came to mind. Since I loved and respected this man, I was left with the feeling that I had shared something very intimate and profound with him and his family, a feeling I retain to this day.

There is no tie more dearly felt than the one between parent and child. Suddenly, without a parent as buffer, we are forced to confront our own mortality. The one who has kept us from painful things can no longer make it all right for us. We are all there is. The sense of grief and abandonment that can accompany the death of a parent is profound. The loving presence of friends can make the sadness more bearable and weave a once-in-a-lifetime memory.  —V. Lang

## ☙ WHAT YOU NEED ❧

- The family and close friends of the deceased
- A place to gather, preferably a home of one of the deceased's children
- A remembrance table
- A candle
- Your parent's favorite meal
- An eloquent song or reading

## ☙ WHAT YOU DO ❧

If you are fortunate enough to be with your parent at the time of death, ask any medical professionals to please give you time alone with your parent. No matter how kind they may be, unless you make this request they will follow protocol, not your needs. If possible, gather the key people in your life and keep a vigil at bedside. Just breathe deeply and sit with the body. Being present as the soul departs the body is an incredible privilege. Stay with your parent as long as you can.

Later, set a time to gather immediate family and close friends in your home or in the home of one of your siblings. Have pictures, favorite objects, and other memorabilia displayed on a remembrance table so everyone can see and handle them. Items on the table may include a musical instrument or favorite sheet music, a wedding photo, a report card, a favorite baseball mitt, or sand from a beach visited on a memorable vacation.

Share your parent's favorite meal together, then move to a comfortable room, sit calmly, light a remembrance candle, and gather for a moment of silent reflection. After this time together feels complete, share a meaningful song or reading with the group, such as "Death Is Nothing at All."

## Death Is Nothing at All

*I have only slipped away into the next room. I am I, and you are you. Whatever we were to each other, that we still are. Call me by my old familiar name, speak to me in the easy way that you always used. Put no difference in your tone, wear no forced air of solemnity or sorrow. Laugh as we always laughed at the little jokes we enjoyed together. Play, smile, think of me, pray for me. Let my name be ever the household word that it always was, let it be spoken without effort, without the trace of a shadow on it. Life means all that it ever meant. It is the same as it ever was; there is unbroken continuity. Why should I be out of mind because I am out of sight? I am waiting for you for an interval somewhere very near, just around the corner. All is well.*

—Henry Scott Holland

Ask each person to recall a memory that has special meaning for her. It is good to include humorous anecdotes to lighten the tone and encourage conversation. Thank those present for the many ways they contributed to the life of the parent, and join hands, closing with these words: "We honor the life of our loved one and will treasure him always in our hearts and in our minds."

If the death follows a long period of suffering, acknowledge the role grown children played in the caretaking and acknowledge the end of that difficult passage, saying, "I release you as you release me; we are free to go forward in love and light."

# The 49 Candles:
# A Ritual after a Death

*Life is a great surprise. I do not see why death should
not be an even greater one. —Vladimir Nabokov*

A very dear member of my family, my Uncle Bush, lived alone
until the age of 91. No one was with him the night he died in
his sleep. At first, I felt very sad because I didn't have the chance
to comfort him and to say goodbye, yet I know that dying
peacefully in his home was exactly what he would have wanted.
Still, I wanted so badly to do something.

In Tibetan thinking, the moment of death is important,
but even more so are the next 7 weeks. After death, the deceased
is thought to pass through the "bardo of becoming," a process
in which he is challenged to move to higher and higher levels
of consciousness. If he has enough support and is able to resist
being drawn back into a physical body, he has the opportunity
to realize complete enlightenment. Those of us who are living
influence this passage by certain breathing practices and by
holding good thoughts of the deceased for the 7 weeks (49 days)
after death. Using the breath, Tibetan monks spend years practicing rituals for the dead.

Whether or not you believe in the bardo or in reincarna-
tion, what a wonderful tribute to someone you love to light a
candle and simply breathe for him as you hold him in mind for
49 days. Whether he is helped you may not know, but *you* most
certainly will be.   —V. Lang

## 🐟 WHAT YOU NEED 🐟

- A calendar
- Two boxes of birthday candles or a single votive candle
- A small candleholder
- Matches

## 🐟 WHAT YOU DO 🐟

Mark on your calendar the day that is 49 days from the date of death. Light one small candle each day until you have reached the 49th day. Just before bed is an easy time to remember; or perhaps at dinner, you can take a moment to remember your loved one.

As you light the candle, fill your mind with positive thoughts of the person. Breathe in anything that may be unfinished or negative in the life of the deceased, and breathe out feelings of joy and release.

# Honoring a Loved Gardener

*Beside a stone three*
*thousand years old: two*
*red poppies of today.*
—Christine M. Krishnasami

My Uncle Bush loved to garden and was never happier than when he was on his knees in his rose bed or planting irises and tulips for spring. When he died, my cousin, John, suggested we divide his purple iris bulbs so each of us would have something living from his garden. I can't think of anything that would have pleased him more.   —V. Lang

## 🐟 WHAT YOU NEED 🐟

- An afternoon
- Bulbs from a loved one's garden

## 🐟 WHAT YOU DO 🐟

Gather the family on a weekend afternoon to dig up the bulbs, at least one for each person. After you remove them, join hands and say, "We take these flowers with gratitude and will remember you in the beauty they bring to life." Every year when they bloom, cut one and place it by a picture of the person who first tended it.

# Honoring a Rich Life: The Remembrance Table

*When I am dead, I hope it may be said:*
*"His sins were scarlet, but his books were read."*
—Hilaire Belloc

I have been privileged to know two fine men whose funerals were truly celebrations of their lives. One was a doctor who originally wanted to be a concert violinist, the other, a distinguished judge who set new standards in our country for the education of judges. In both cases, the daughters of these men created remembrance tables displaying artifacts from their fathers' lives that were rich with the many contributions the men had made to the world as well as with items of personal humor.

Some of the items included a treatise on the education of judges, a much-loved fishing hat, and an unstrung violin bow. At each funeral, the items were a way for those present to relate to one another and compare notes on the many interesting aspects of the deceased's life. Wonderful memories came forth, and many warm smiles of recognition.

When a good life comes to an end, it is important to celebrate all of it, rather than dwelling on the circumstances of the person's final months, often a time of illness and sadness. In collecting the items, those grieving have a sensual experience of their deep feelings through the ritual handling of items that bring back red-letter days, familiar tastes and smells, and family high points of all kinds.  —V. Lang

## ➣ WHAT YOU NEED ➣

- An attractive table with a vase of flowers
- Special objects from the life of the loved one who has died
- A camera

## ➣ WHAT YOU DO ➣

The day before the funeral or memorial service, arrange a table in the home or place where the group will gather after the service, labeling and displaying carefully selected items from the life of the deceased. Ask each person to be certain to visit the table, and station a knowledgeable family member at its side to interpret the items and answer questions. Be sure to photograph the collection before it is dispersed among relatives.

# The Anniversary
## of a Death

*A thief stole my precious jewels*
*in the black ink of night—*
*without a sound, gone forever,*
*diamonds without equal.*
*—Virginia Lang*

Every year around the anniversary of my parents' deaths, I go through an emotional spin cycle. In March 1992, my mother died suddenly; 6 weeks later, my father followed her—both without warning. Now, when March rolls around, if I don't mentally prepare for it, I get knocked over by a wave of emotion. I had thought the grief I felt over the death of my mother and father would eventually play out like a hurricane downgraded to occasional showers; but instead, it seems to knock me over again and again.

For many months after my parents died, I cut three Joseph's coat roses from my garden and made a small memorial to them every Thursday (the day I clean the house). One rose was for my mother, one was for my father, and the third rose was for a close friend killed in a skiing accident in New Zealand some years ago. This small gesture, week after week, brought me great comfort; and in its week-by-week continuity, it helped to soften the suddenness and shock of all three deaths.   —V. Lang

## ◖◗ WHAT YOU NEED ◖◗

- A calendar
- A photo of the loved one who has died
- A flower and vase

## ◖◗ WHAT YOU DO ◖◗

Mark the date of a significant death on your calendar well in advance. When the anniversary draws near, take out a picture of the person and place a small vase with a beautiful flower near it.

You may want to do this for just the day of the anniversary or for a longer period. If you like, add a small votive candle as well. When I was keeping up the ritual, I particularly liked searching for just the right rose for each person, reflecting on each person's personality as I made my choice. Be kind to yourself and take time for personal reflection and solitude as the date approaches.

# An AIDS Death

*The agony of dying is over. You have been born again,*
*pulled back through the tunnel of life, pulled through*
*darkness into light. —Louise Nayer*

One day, my husband and I got a call from our friend Laura. "I have AIDS," she said from a telephone at San Francisco General Hospital. Just 2 days before, I sat with her in a cafe while she told me of plans to go to Europe with her new love, Michael.

Soon after the diagnosis, Michael moved in with Laura, and he cared for her for the next 2½ years, until her death. She was the only woman on the AIDS ward at that time—and there was still a lot of fear surrounding AIDS and how it spread. She was fortunate, though, to not be cut off from her family, who after the initial shock, rallied to her bedside in her illness. In addition to her loving partner, Laura had many friends who visited her regularly.

Her spirit—which kept everyone so inspired for so long—prevailed even in death. Michael quickly got together an impromptu ceremony attended by everyone invited. Fifty people crowded into their living room the Wednesday after her death. Friends and family grieve in their own, often private, ways, but this was a moving ceremony that gave both groups of people a chance to be together and the opportunity to see more of Laura's life, even in death.   —L. Nayer

## 🐟 WHAT YOU NEED 🐟

- *A remembrance table*
- *The favorite music of the deceased (in this case, it was a*

piece that Michael, a musician, had composed for Laura)
- Friends and family
- Poetry or other words about the person who has died
- A blank book in which people can write their thoughts, feelings, and memories, to be given to a loved one as a keepsake
- Potluck dishes provided by friends

## 🐟 WHAT YOU DO 🐟

Create a remembrance table set up to express the loved one's life, including pictures from childhood to the present, favorite things like sand from a beach, childhood treasures, favorite books, creative projects, awards, and honors with family and friends so that many of the pieces of the person's life are intertwined. This also creates unity and new friendships among those who loved the person who has died.

Play the person's favorite music as people enter. Ask one person to serve as a guide for the evening and to give everyone a chance to talk through words, poetry, and song. Encourage people to speak about the deceased and to share precious memories with each other. Also encourage them to write a passage in the keepsake book

Hopefully, members of the family and the friends will talk and eat together, sharing phone numbers and continuing to keep in touch and offer each other support. Let hugs abound and tears flow.

# HOLIDAYS

As adults looking back on our lives, most of us remember holidays best of all, the pauses between work and school, the scents, the warm-oven smells, the ancient prayers and silent moments in places of worship, and the gatherings of relatives and friends. In the fall, we see the trees begin to shed their leaves; and as winter descends, we welcome light into our homes. When spring arrives, we reclaim the green earth and its fields of wild flowers as nature blankets the earth in sunlight and blossoms.

In this section, we offer versions of time-honored and ancient celebrations and the ideas of friends who celebrate holidays from many different traditions throughout the world. We also offer nontraditional holiday celebrations for families as well as single people.

Though many of us no longer live in direct contact with the earth, we still long to be in harmony with its rhythms and seasons and to take time to welcome the sacred parts of life into our hearts.

# New Year's Eve

*Our life is passages, going from one door to the next.*
*Sometimes we're afraid to go forward and afraid to*
*look back. But it is actually one long tunnel of hidden*
*rooms, full of light and dark, many doors closing*
*and many doors opening. —Louise Nayer*

There are many calendars that are followed throughout the world. But the one we're familiar with is based on the calendar that in which Julius Caesar designated January 1 as the first day of the year.

Janus (whose name is the root of January) is a Roman god portrayed with two faces. One face looks backward toward the old year, and the other face looks toward the new year. In his right hand, Janus holds a key that can close the door of the old year and open the door of the new year. On January 1, many of us also feel the need to close doors on what has gone before and think about what is to come.

New Year's Eve parties can be exciting—the glitter, the glitz, the ball dropping on Times Square. If you are with one you love, even better. But for many people, there is little depth of feeling in marking the new year. The only changes become simple ones, buying a new calendar or changing the date on a check. Here are two rituals that can be done on New Year's Eve to add meaning to the new year.

## 🐟 WHAT YOU NEED 🐟

- *Close friends or family members who will stick with you throughout the year*
- *Pens and paper*

- *A hat*
- *Potluck dishes provided by everyone*

## 🐟 WHAT YOU DO 🐟

Ask each friend and family member to write down one change he would like to make in his life: "I would like to accept my mother this year for all she is and let go of past hurts." "I want to stop fighting with my teenage son." "I would like to get in shape and go on my first mountain climbing expedition." Sign your name to it.

After everyone has written something, put all changes in a hat. Have each person choose a change out of the hat and agree to be a coach for the person whose change they pick. The coach should check in at least once a month to help that person achieve his goal. The coach needs to do some research. "How can I help so-and-so accept her mother? Are there books that might help?" "In what way can I help what's-his-name get in shape? Are there inexpensive gyms nearby? A particularly good tape to buy?"

When everyone is matched up with a coach, agree that the group will meet at the same time next year. It is important that what is emphasized is trying your best and that results might vary. End the evening by saying, "We support one another as we work toward our goals for the new year." The following poem can also be read to end the evening.

> The shape of courage
> is round as your eyes.
> It sees to summits, to lacy clouds, to other worlds.
> The sound of courage is deep
> a tunnel of birth and death
> a tunnel of pitch dark and light.

It is slippery
and filled with a thousand wings.
The heart of courage is small
as a finger
the way you hold your pen
the blood circulating,
in small spaces.
It is always there
like the air
like memory bringing us back
to where we can hold on
and see the fireflies,
that light the way.

  —Louise Nayer

# Children's New Year

*My life turns like a spinning top, I am dancing in a
dress of ribbons. What are my colors? Where do I stop?
What will I be tomorrow?* —Louise Nayer

New Year's Eve can be abstract for children because children
measure time by the school year and not by the Gregorian calendar. Explain to them why we use this system to measure time
and why New Year's Eve marks a new beginning for everyone.

## 🐟 WHAT YOU NEED 🐟

- A quiet time on New Year's Eve or New Year's Day
- Pieces of different-colored ribbons
- A dowel or long stick

## 🐟 WHAT YOU DO 🐟

Ask your child to pick aspects of her life that are important to her and that she wants to weave into the year to come.
Let her pick a color that represents her desires, for instance,
red for strength to do her best in sports or green for courage
to make new friends. Help her wrap a red ribbon around part of
the dowel or stick. Let her tie it to other pieces of ribbon to be
tied around the stick to represent other desires, until you have
a multicolored stick. Hang it where your child will see it every
day. She does not need to tell anyone of her wishes or desires.

# The Time Capsule: An Annual Tradition for Families

*Every instant of time is a pinprick of eternity.*
*—Marcus Aurelius Antoninus*

My new friends Peter and Peggy Federico told me that every year for more than 20 years, their family has kept a time capsule to remember the highlights of the year gone by. Every year, on the last day of December, each child takes a large index card and writes the answers to these questions.

How old are you now?
How tall are you now?
What grade are you in?
Who are your favorite friends?
What is your favorite song?
What was your favorite movie this year?
Who do you most admire?
What is your favorite color?
What was your best moment? Worst moment?
What was your biggest surprise?
What are your hopes for next year?

All the answers are kept in a large popcorn tin and read the next year on New Year's Eve. This has become a treasured family tradition in the Federico family and an excellent record of the children's growth. —V. Lang

## WHAT YOU NEED

- A list of questions
- Index cards and pens
- A popcorn tin

## WHAT YOU DO

Develop your own list of questions or borrow this one and ask each member of the family to complete the questions on an index card. They need not share their responses with each other. Put the responses in the time capsule popcorn tin or some other airtight container to be read the next year on New Year's Eve.

# Celebrating the New Year with a Chinese Tradition

*Kung She Fa Tsai! [Happy New Year!]*
*—Chinese translation*

My daughter's name, YuWen, means "abundance and literature" or "rich culture," depending on your interpretation of the Chinese characters. In our family, we are learning to observe some of the celebrations that are time-honored traditions in China and to respect her rich heritage.

I particularly like the way Chinese families welcome the New Year—visiting family, preparing ritual foods, and abstaining from work on days held sacred. Families take red cloths and hang words of hope for good luck, good health, and prosperity upside down on the front doors of their homes to indicate that the virtues or wishes they express will soon arrive in the homes.   —V. Lang

## ➤ WHAT YOU NEED ➤

- *A gold marker*
- *A red cloth*
- *The front door of your home*

## ➤ WHAT YOU DO ➤

*Think of your good wishes and hopes for the year ahead. They may be hopes for yourself, your family, or the world. Some* examples are "We hope to travel someplace special this year. We hope Grandmother will enjoy good health this year. We hope the world will be at peace this year."

Letting each person in the household be free to write without judgment or comment, write the hopes in gold on the red cloth. You may prefer to write the individual expressions of hope on small pieces of fabric and sew those pieces onto the larger cloth. Hang the cloth upside down on the front door. Save the red cloth from each year as a family tradition.

# Valentine's Day without a Valentine

*Oh life is a glorious cycle of song,*
*A medley of extemporanea:*
*And love is a thing that can never go wrong,*
*And I am Marie of Roumania.*
—Dorothy Parker

The trouble with holidays that celebrate the wonderful times in our lives is that they can painfully underscore the absence of such times from our lives! Many of us have experienced a Valentine's Day when there has been little romance or passion, or one in which our love for another was unrequited. Unfortunately, there are no magic potions for matters of the heart, but there is an antidote to spending Valentine's Day in a funk.

## WHAT YOU NEED

- A hospital or nursing home
- Red carnations
- A person living alone, perhaps a student away at college, a soldier in the military, or an elder member of the family
- A handmade card

## WHAT YOU DO

Become the secret Valentine for someone else. Here are some simple ways.

Go to a hospital or nursing home near you with a bunch

of red carnations. Tie onto each carnation a handwritten note, "Happy Valentine's Day from a secret admirer." Place one on each doorstep or mailbox (call ahead and get enough for an entire unit or suite so no one is left out). Hospitals have chart slots on the doors that make delivery easy. Taking a child along will make this especially fun.

If you know someone who is alone or far from home this year, create a special card with a timeless sentiment like the one below from the Song of Solomon. Sign it simply, "From a secret admirer." The recipient is sure to be intrigued and spend pleasant hours of happy imaginings!

## Song of Songs

*I am my lover's and he desires me.*
*Come, my darling,*
*let us go out into the fields*
*and spend the night in villages.*
*Let us wake early and go to the vineyards*
*and see if the vine is in blossom,*
*if the new grape bud is open*
*and the pomegranates in bloom.*
*There I will give you my love.*
*The mandrakes will spray aroma*
*and over our door will be precious fruit,*
*new and old,*
*which I have saved for you, my darling.*
   —*The Song of Solomon 7:10–13*

# Valentine's Day for a Favorite Elder

*Come live with me and be my love*
*And we will all the pleasures prove.*
—Christopher Marlowe

My 95-year-old Aunt Margaret loves poetry and can recite many wonderful romantic poems from her youth. Sadly, few of us memorize poetry anymore. Somehow, it has gone the way of so many elegant and gracious practices.   —V. Lang

## 🐟 WHAT YOU NEED 🐟

- A poem
- A flower

## 🐟 WHAT YOU DO 🐟

If you have a very special older person in your life, consider a wonderfully old-fashioned way to deliver a special Valentine message—call to announce that a secret admirer is coming, go reveal yourself, and recite this beautiful Christopher Marlowe poem, one perfect rose in hand!

### The Passionate Shepherd to His Love
*Come live with me and be my love,*
*And we will all the pleasures prove,*
*That valleys, groves, hills, and fields,*
*Woods or sleepy mountain yields.*

And we will sit upon the rocks,
Seeing the shepherds feed their flocks,
By shallow rivers, to whose falls
Melodious birds sing madrigals.

And I will make thee beds of roses
And a thousand fragrant posies;
A cap of flowers, and a kirtle
Embroidered all with leaves of myrtle.

A gown made of the finest wool,
Which from our pretty lambs we pull;
Fair lined slippers for the cold,
With buckles of the purest gold.

A belt of straw and ivy buds,
With coral clasps and amber studs;
And if these pleasures may thee move,
Come live with me and be my love.

—Christopher Marlowe

# Valentine's Day
# for a Sensitive Single

*Ask me*
*Why I stay*
*On Green Mountain?*
*I smile*
*And do not answer,*
*My heart is at ease.*
*Peach blossoms*
*On flowing water*
*Slip away*
*Into the distance—*
*This is another world*
*Which is not of men.*
*—Li Bai*

Louise and I have a mutual friend, Jim Eilers, who is a gifted poet and artist. He is also YuWen's godfather. As a single man, he often dreads conventional holidays because they leave little room for his perceptions of life and his way of knowing and feeling. Valentine's Day can be especially rough for him.

When I asked him what he does for Valentine's Day, he said, "On Valentine's Day, rather than being with someone I love, I do what I love: I write!" While writing may not work for everyone, each of us has a love, something that completely engages us, that transports us to another place in ourselves and awakens feelings of self-love and self-worth.   —V. Lang

## 🐟 WHAT YOU NEED 🐟

- Time alone
- A place to pursue your love
- Andrea Marcovicci's beautiful vocal work "New Words" or similar beautiful music

## 🐟 WHAT YOU DO 🐟

Let yourself be free of societal messages about love and simply be alone in a comfortable place. Breathe deeply, listen to Andrea Marcovicci, and follow the calling of your heart as you write, paint, sculpt, work in wood, whatever pleases you. Offer what you create as a Valentine gift of love for yourself or to someone else who lives alone.

# Rite of Spring

*This morning the green fists of the peonies are getting ready*
*to break my heart . . .*
*—Mary Oliver*

Spring explodes in Pennsylvania. It comes with an urgency and a will that is unstoppable. Ready or not, it spews forth armloads of brilliant forsythia, then scarlet azaleas, lavender rhododendrons, milky-white dogwood, and deep-grape Siberian irises.

In springtime, life pours from the earth without our having to do anything. It is a wonderful time to remember that we are not in control of nature, yet we are part of it. We deserve to be here just as much as the trees and flowers, not dominating the natural world but in a state of conscious participation with it.   —V. Lang

## 🐟 WHAT YOU NEED 🐟

- *A place of privacy outdoors*
- *A copy of the poem "White Flowers" by Mary Oliver*

## 🐟 WHAT YOU DO 🐟

*Find a comfortable spot to lie facedown on the ground. Let your body fully relax as it blends with the earth, and simply lie quietly, feeling the dynamic, life-giving power that lies below you. In Peru, the Q'ero Indians observe a practice that includes letting your navel come into direct contact with the ground to meld with the earth that can be considered the navel of creation. This simple, childlike posture can offer a profound expe-*

rience of connection and peace. Stay as long as you like and breathe deeply.

Just before bed, read "White Flowers" by Mary Oliver. Her beautiful words will help you to sleep well and savor the magnificent gift that is spring.

### White Flowers
—Mary Oliver

Last night
in the fields
I lay down in the darkness
to think about death,
but instead I fell asleep,
as if in a vast and sloping room
filled with those white flowers
that open all summer,
sticky and untidy,
in the warm fields.
When I woke
the morning light was just slipping
in front of the stars,
and I was covered
with blossoms.
I don't know
how it happened—
I don't know
if my body went diving down
under the sugary vines
in some sleep-sharpened affinity
with the depths, or whether
that green energy

rose like a wave
and curled over me, claiming me
in its husky arms.
I pushed them away, but I didn't rise.
Never in my life had I felt so plush,
or so slippery,
or so resplendently empty.
Never in my life
had I felt myself so near
that porous line
where my own body was done with
and the roots and the stems and the flowers
began.

# Memorial Day: Observing Our Relationship with War

*They shall beat their swords into plowshares,*
*and their spears into pruninghooks: nation shall*
*not lift up sword against nation, neither shall*
*they learn war anymore.* —Isaiah 2:4

Theologian Matthew Fox says, "War is man's imagination gone mad without the balance of his compassion." Throughout the course of history, across time and culture, we have defaulted to war when fear of "the other" has closed our hearts to our shared humanity, when our imagination has gone mad.

On a day set aside to remember men and women who fought for their ideals, their countries, their families, how do we honor those who have gone before and whose sacrifice has contributed to the lives we enjoy today, while moving beyond war as a means of resolving conflict? Perhaps the mad side of our imagination needs a different way to express itself.

## ⮞ WHAT YOU NEED ⮜

- *One hour alone*
- *A pencil and paper*

## ⮞ WHAT YOU DO ⮜

Write down the names of people you admire in history who died for an idea. They may be world leaders like Mahatma

Gandhi or Martin Luther King Jr., or they may be friends or family members who fought in a war. Explore what you admire about them: What was the message of their lives that is still important today?

Consider what you might do to further their work toward a world at peace. Here is a list of some possible short-term actions follows to start your thinking process.

- Examine the violence in yourself.
- Make peace with someone with whom you are "at war."
- Donate to Doctors Without Borders, the Red Cross, or another international relief agency.
- Write letters of support for Amnesty International.
- Help support a refugee family with your time, money, or professional expertise.
- Gather your family in a circle, light a candle for peace, and observe a moment of silence together at your annual Memorial Day picnic.

# Fourth of July: A Celebration of Freedom

*Man's capacity for justice makes democracy
possible; but man's inclination to injustice makes
democracy necessary.* —Reinhold Niebuhr

Last Fourth of July, we took our daughter, YuWen, to her first fireworks at Penn's Landing in Philadelphia. As I stood in the shadow of Independence Hall with my Chinese child, watching a celebration of American freedom, tears came to my eyes as I thought of the delicious ironies—here she was in the city of my birth, free to be and to do whatever she likes, marking this freedom with firecrackers invented in China.

My mind drifted to a day when, from this same landing, my grandmother's sister, Anna, was forced to set sail for her native Ireland. She loved America and wanted to stay but had to leave because she was engaged to marry. Boarding the ship brokenhearted, she grew so ill on the passage home that she died in Ireland on her wedding day. As an American citizen, my daughter, whose full name is Anna YuWen, will have the freedom that her namesake, Anna Purser, did not.

On a day of great festivity, full of family picnics and sparklers, it is important that we, who have the privilege to live in a country that prizes freedom and religious tolerance, keep our awareness and gratitude for the gift of citizenship alive. May this holiday inspire us to work harder for justice in our country and in the world.   —V. Lang

## ➤ WHAT YOU NEED ➤

- A group of family or friends
- Four sparklers

## ➤ WHAT YOU DO ➤

When it is very dark, gather the group in a circle. Choose four people to light freedom sparklers.

The first person should say, "We light this flame as grateful citizens of a free nation."

The second should say, "We light this flame for all the peoples of the world who do not live in freedom."

The third person, a veteran if possible, should say, "We light this flame for all who have given their lives for freedom and justice."

The fourth person should then say, "We light this flame as a symbol of hope for greater social justice in our country and freedom in the world."

If you know a new citizen or someone in the process of becoming one, invite him to join you. Light a fifth sparkler in his honor, with the words, "We salute you in your commitment to become a citizen of this country." Be sure to include older members of the family in this celebration, especially if there is one who has served in a war. Ask him to read the poem "In Flanders Fields."

### In Flanders Fields

In Flanders fields the poppies blow
Between the crosses, row on row,
That mark our place; and in the sky
The larks, still bravely singing, fly
Scarce heard amid the guns below.

*We are the Dead, short days ago*
*We lived, felt dawn, saw sunset glow,*
*Loved and were loved, and now we lie,*
*In Flanders fields.*
*Take up our quarrel with the foe:*
*To you from failing hands we throw*
*The torch; be yours to hold it high.*
*If ye break faith with us who die*
*We shall not sleep, though poppies grow*
*In Flanders fields.*

   —Lieutenant Colonel John McCrae, M.D.

When the reader finishes, ask each person to observe a moment of silence to think about what it means to "break faith" with those who died for freedom.

# Harvest Moon Festival

*She opens her window*
*To the autumn moon's light.*
*She puts out the candle*
*And slips off her silken skirt.*
*Softly she smiles*
*Within the curtains of her bed.*
*She raises her body—*
*An orchid fragrance spreads.*
*—Anonymous,*
*Six Dynasties Period (A.D. 300–600)*

One of the most festive occasions in China is the August or Harvest Moon Festival. It celebrates the reunion of the Moon Goddess, who lives in the moon, with her husband, who lives in the sun. She has been banished to the moon because she stole the peach of immortality from her husband. One night a year, the night of the first full moon of autumn, she is permitted to join him.

In China, families dress in colorful costumes for this occasion and hold elaborate celebrations. An actor dressed as the Moon Goddess does a ritual dance under the brilliant moon; and all beings, living and dead, connect through the moon, which acts as a kind of radio transmitter.

In all cultures and times, the moon has always held a fascination for us. It is an intriguing thought that no matter where we are on Earth, we can communicate with kindred spirits through the golden light of the harvest moon.

## 🐟 WHAT YOU NEED 🐟

- A group of friends or family
- The first full moon of autumn
- Moon cakes and jasmine tea

## 🐟 WHAT YOU DO 🐟

Go outdoors and look up at the moon together, thinking of all those living and dead who have gazed or have yet to gaze at the timeless moon. Send a silent message to someone far away, to be transmitted by the moon.

If you have young children, read aloud the beautiful children's book *The Moon Lady* by Amy Tan. A dancer in the family may choose to dress up and dance the part of the Moon Goddess as the story is read.

Share moon cakes and tea. If you live near a city that has a Chinese market, you can buy moon cakes at this time of year, or you may want to bake a simple moon-shaped cookie of your own.

# Thanksgiving for a Couple: Turkey for Two

*Do you carrot all for me?*
*My heart beets for you,*
*With your turnip nose*
*And your radish face,*
*You are a peach.*
*If we cantaloupe,*
*Lettuce marry;*
*Weed make a swell pear.*
*—Anonymous*

The first Thanksgiving my husband and I shared was indeed memorable. We were with a group of 22 people, all of whom, including us, were strangers to each other. We sat on the floor and the Thanksgiving meal was served Tom Jones style: We fed each other, laughing at the simple pleasure that this brought to the celebration, and all awkwardness began to disappear. The group quickly dispensed with small talk, giving itself over to real merriment and gratitude for the food and each other.

When a bride and groom feed each other the first piece of wedding cake, each is symbolically offering to nurture the other. Thanksgiving is a wonderful time for two people to renew their commitment to "feed" one another through this joyful and very intimate rite of gratitude.   —V. Lang

## ◈ WHAT YOU NEED ◈

- A low table and pillows
- Lots of napkins
- A festive meal
- Finger bowls with fresh lemon slices

## ◈ WHAT YOU DO ◈

Get comfortable on the pillows, join hands, and say your holiday blessing or, for fun, the poem on the opposite page. Eat the Thanksgiving meal Tom Jones style, each person feeding the other using hands only, using the napkins and dipping in the lemon finger bowls as needed.

# Thanksgiving with Children

*Be not forgetful to entertain strangers: for thereby some
have entertained angels unawares.* —Hebrews 13:2

The spirit of Thanksgiving can be difficult for children to understand. Do little children have any real connection with pilgrims
and the Mayflower or the significance of these people sharing a
meal with Native Americans?

It may be that a living demonstration is needed to make
the point, with someone who is unknown joining the family
table and expanding the meaning of family and inclusion.

## 🐟 WHAT YOU NEED 🐟

- *The name of someone who may not have local relatives,
  someone living alone, a single-parent family, or a family
  with few resources*
- *An invitation*
- *Craft supplies for handmade place mats and placecards*

## 🐟 WHAT YOU DO 🐟

Ask your child to write out an invitation asking the
chosen person or family to join you and your family at the
Thanksgiving table. Deliver the invitation by hand and be sure
to offer transportation to and from the gathering.

Make a festive mat and placecard for each person, taking
care to correctly spell the names of your invited guests. As the

meal is served, ask the youngest reader to offer a family prayer or to read the following prayer.

## The Iroquois Thanksgiving Prayer

> We return thanks to our mother, the earth
> which sustains us . . .
> to the wind, which moves the air that banishes disease . . .
> to our grandfather Creator who has
> protected his grandchildren and has given
> to us his rain . . . to the sun that has looked
> upon the earth with a beneficent eye.

Afterward, ask everyone to join hands and say, "We give thanks for this meal and the chance to share it together." Extend a warm message of welcome to the guests, and enjoy the gathering!

# Hanukkah

*Sometimes the whole sky turns into an otherworldly Hanukkah lamp, with the stars as its lights. I told my dreams to a rabbi and he said, "Love comes from the soul and souls radiate light." —Isaac Bashevis Singer*

Though my father is Jewish, our family did not celebrate the Jewish holidays. It was only after my daughter Sarah attended the Jewish community center and announced, "We need to buy a Hanukkah menorah" that we began to celebrate the holiday. Many interfaith couples celebrate this festival, and there are many occasions where non-Jews are invited to the homes of Jewish people to share in this time and to think about how all human beings can become free from oppressive governments and persecution.

Hanukkah lasts 8 days and is usually celebrated in December. It commemorates the struggle of the Jews against the Syrian-Greeks. After the Jews' victory, they returned to their city of Jerusalem to restore the partially destroyed Temple. At the Temple, the Jews found only one small cruse of oil to light the eternal light. By some miracle, the oil lasted for 8 days, time enough to procure more oil. The light never went out. It was proclaimed a miracle, to be commemorated every year.

Though it is not a major holiday, Hanukkah is celebrated widely because of its proximity to Christmas and because of its message, that all people should be free to worship in peace.   —L. Nayer

## ➤ WHAT YOU NEED ➤

- Nine candles
- A Hanukkah menorah
- Friends or family
- Paper and pens
- Food made with oil, such as jelly donuts or potato latkes
- A dreidel
- Gelt (chocolate coins wrapped in gold foil—the gold represents light)

## ➤ WHAT YOU DO ➤

At sundown, after dinner, use a helper candle to light the candle on the far-right side of the menorah. Most families say, either in Hebrew or English, the prayer "Blessed are You, Lord our God, King of the Universe, Who has sanctified us with His commandments and commanded us to kindle the light of Hanukkah."

Each night for the next 7 nights, light one more candle, continuing to go from right to left. If you wish, place the Hanukkah menorah in the window, for all to see.

On a big piece of paper, write out the word *freedom*. Ask everyone, including the children, to write, "I feel free when.... I can work for freedom in the world by...."

Hang up the sheet of paper as a reminder of the work we need to do to create peace in the world for all people. Eat the fried food and play dreidel with the kids.

### Instructions for Playing Dreidel

The game dreidel began when Jews were forbidden to study Torah, the Jewish Bible. Boys would study together secretly, and when they heard the footsteps of soldiers, they pulled out spinning tops and pretended to be playing games. Though children in the past carved their own wooden dreidels, now the toys can be bought in many stores. The dreidel has four sides, each side inscribed with the letter *nun, gimmel, he,* or *shin,* which mean "A great miracle happened there."

All players are given an equal number of gelt, or they may use raisins, candies, or any objects they choose. To begin, each player takes five objects from her pile and puts them into a common pile. Then, everyone takes a turn spinning the dreidel. When the spin lands on *nun,* it means do nothing; on *gimmel,* take the common pile; on *he,* take half the common pile; and on *shin,* give half of the spinner's pile. When a player has nothing left to give, she is out of the game. The player who still has a pile when everyone else is out is the winner.

# Day of the Dead

*Death was not the natural end of life but one phase of
an infinite cycle.* —Octavio Paz

The Mexican Day of the Dead is an ancient festival, transformed
from the original celebration into one that coincides with a
Christian holiday, All Hallows' Eve. Families visit gravesites,
picnic on the grass, and place brightly colored flowers on the
graves. It is a time to remember, to tell stories about the dead,
and a time to feast.

In San Francisco's Mission District, you can buy small
sugar skulls and dioramas filled with dancing skeletons. Sometimes, people buy special bread filled with a plastic toy skeleton
to offer to the dead.

Whether you are honoring a close friend, a relative, or
anyone incredibly precious to you who has passed away, this
ritual may help you reconnect with that person and with what
touched you so deeply about her life.

Though the Mexican celebration is around Halloween, you
can also remember a loved one each year on the anniversary of
her death.

## ❧ WHAT YOU NEED ❧

- A small table
- A tablecloth
- A vase and brightly colored flowers
- Photographs of your loved one or other memorabilia
  such as pieces of clothing
- A small basket

- *Festive music*
- *Your loved one's favorite food or a loaf of bread*
- *A candle*
- *Blank index cards and colored pens*
- *A photo album*

## 🐟 WHAT YOU DO 🐟

Before dinner on November 1st or on the anniversary of you loved one's death, set up a special table anywhere you choose. Make sure to involve children in the preparations. Cover the table with a colorful cloth. Place a vase with flowers in the center and arrange the photos and other keepsakes around the flowers. Place the small, empty basket near the flowers.

After dinner, play music. Dance, if you like! Put out a small portion of the deceased's favorite food. Turn the lights down in the room, light the candle, and say what you loved about the person. Afterward, write notes on the index cards and place them in the basket. You may continue to write notes over the next few days or as long as the special table is in place. Later, you can keep the messages in a photo album, along with photos of your loved one. In the Chinese tradition, family "altars" are often kept up permanently.

This Day of the Dead is a festive celebration of life and of all that those who have passed gave to you when they were alive.

# Winter Solstice

*It is the darkest day of the year*
*when we fold into ourselves*
*like feathered birds*
*gazing at the inside*
*of a candle flame,*
*at the small sparks of humanity,*
*the place of light.*
—Louise Nayer

The winter solstice is celebrated on December 21, the shortest day of the year. Long ago, people feared that the sunlight would not come back and shine on the Earth again. They began the tradition of burning Yule logs to help bring back the light.

In celebrating the solstice, we celebrate the seasons of change and honor mother Earth. Here are two rituals, one to be done with family and one to be done alone on the night of December 21 to remember the light that will come back and eventually turn the barren earth into fields of green.

## ◖◗ WHAT YOU NEED ◖◗

- Friends or family gathered together
- Log in a fireplace, if possible
- Candles with holders
- Music
- Cookies or cake with poppy or sesame seeds
- Hot cider

# ❧ WHAT YOU DO ❧

If you have a fireplace, gather around and light a log. Turn out all the lights in the house and sit in darkness, asking everyone to think about the light and look into the fire. If you don't have a fireplace, everyone can look into the flame of a large candle. Ask even the children to be silent for a minute or two.

During this time of silence, ask everyone to think for a couple of minutes about what has passed this year and what is to come in the new year. Tell the children to focus on how they overcame problems and difficulties during the past year and how the adults will be there to help them fulfill their hopes and dreams for the new year.

Go around the room and ask everyone to offer a wish for the Earth: "I hope the trees will get enough sunlight this year" or "I hope the birds return to Glen Park Canyon when spring comes."

Then, pass out small candles with holders. Ask one child to light his candle. Pass the light around from one person to the next. Put music on. After all the candles are lit, say, "Let our light shine inside us and outside us through the darkness of winter."

Blow out the candles, turn on the lights, and serve the cookies or cakes, their seeds symbolizing new life. Drink hot cider and decide to do something individually or together to replenish the Earth in the next year.

After the children have gone to bed, the adults can stay up until midnight to more fully experience the darkness. Consider the words of the following prayer.

## Prayer to the Sun

*Who among men and all creatures*
*Could live without the Sun Father?*
*For his light brings day, warms and*
*gladdens the Earth Mother with rain,*
*Which flows forth the water we drink.*
*And that causes the flesh of the*
*Earth Mother to yield seeds abundantly.*
　　—*Zuni tribe*

# Heartfelt Christmas

*I made the frame for you and painted it the color
blue. It is your favorite hue. I made the frame
especially for you and filled it with me,
smiling back at you. —Louise Nayer*

Christmas presents appear in stores the minute Thanksgiving
ends, sometimes even before. As consumers, we are bombarded
with advertisements about expensive gifts that many of us can't
afford and don't really want. Over the past 15 years, as my family
has struggled with our budget, Christmas has been especially
difficult. Though we want to continue giving the children of our
family and friends one or two presents that they really want, we
have now modified Christmas so that we make presents for
the adults.

It's important to remember, also, that many people simply
cannot afford expensive items and that making gifts is an hon-
orable and more memorable solution to the blues resulting
from overspending. This year in my family, we gave photos to
each other. In contrast to gifts stuffed in drawers or never worn,
the photos are proudly displayed on our bookshelf and the
bookshelves of our friends and family.   —L. Nayer

## ⬥ WHAT YOU NEED ⬥

- *A decision to do the heartfelt Christmas and to notify
  all involved*
- *Many ideas for simple-to-make gifts*
- *Creative ways of giving of yourself*

## 🐟 WHAT YOU DO 🐟

Because making gifts takes a lot more time than shopping, pick one day each weekend starting in October to create your gifts. Two hours are sufficient each weekend and must be planned on the calendar.

Here are some ideas for gifts.

- Take photos and frame the pictures. You can also paint the frame and decorate them by gluing seashells, buttons, ribbons, and glitter on them. Frame photos of friends or family. Start early with taking the photos.

- Do what you do best. I write poetry, so I have often given gifts of my poems printed on thick cream-colored paper and framed. My husband loves to sculpt. Last year, he sculpted white porcelain Christmas tree ornaments. My daughters both like to make jewelry and have made many presents of necklaces and earrings.

- Prepare food. Everyone loves to get a tin of homemade cookies or a loaf of homemade bread. These can be cooked early in the season and kept frozen, then placed in a decorative tin.

- On a handmade card, offer to perform a service, such as a neck massage, a day to clean and paint, or a lunch out.

- For some people who might not want gifts, offer to do community service in honor of that person, helping in a soup kitchen, reading stories to seriously ill children, or organizing a neighborhood cleanup of a park. All ages can be involved.

# Kwanzaa

*May the principles of Kwanzaa reinforce the values of
our families and keep all of our children, those of the
womb and those of the heart, safe. —Jessica Harris*

Kwanzaa is a relatively new African-American holiday incor-
porating African customs. In 1966 after the Watts riot in California, Dr. Maulana Karenga, a graduate student at the time,
developed this holiday as a way to help heal the devastation
that surrounded the riot and to help African-Americans join
together in community to celebrate their strengths and their
past. Kwanzaa is now celebrated in many homes across the
country and is based on seven principles of life.

My daughter's friend Elizabeth Strong wanted her mother
to celebrate Kwanzaa, much as my daughter Sarah wanted to
celebrate Hanukkah. Like many families, they have modified the
ritual to fit their lifestyle and needs. This celebration has opened
up communication about their heritage and the important
Africans and African-Americans who have made great contributions to humanity.   —L. Nayer

## ➤ WHAT YOU NEED ➤

- *A mat, the mkeka, preferably fabric from Africa, to
  symbolize the foundation of the holiday*
- *A candleholder, the kinara, which holds seven
  candles*

- One black candle in the center of the kinara, three red candles on the left, symbolizing struggle, and three green candles on the right, symbolizing hope
- One special cup, the kikombe cha umoja, which is often a gourd or a wooden chalice
- A drink of your choice
- Gifts, the zawadi, such as books or handmade gifts that are thoughtfully chosen to educate
- Good food

## 🐟 WHAT YOU DO 🐟

Kwanzaa is celebrated for 7 days, beginning on December 26, with each day representing a different principle: *umoja*, unity; *kujichagulia*, self-determination; *ujima*, collective work and responsibility; *ujamaa*, cooperative economics; *nia*, purpose; *kuumba*, creativity; and finally, *imani*, faith.

On the first day, light the black candle, pass the special cup with a drink from person to person (people may pretend to sip), and discuss unity and the Africans and African-Americans who have worked for that goal. Adults can bring biographical information to the children, and the children can ask questions.

On subsequent days, light each of the appropriate candles on the kinara and discuss and honor the corresponding principle.

On the second day, light the black candle and the first of the red candles, the candle of kujichagulia.

The third day, light the black candle, the first red candle, and the second red candle—the candle of ujamaa.

On the fourth day, light the black candle and all three red candles, including the one for kuumba.

The fifth day, light the black candle and all of the red candles, plus the first green candle for the first time—the candle for ujima.

On the sixth day, light the next green candle, which is the candle of nia.

On the last day, light all of the candles, including the last green candle, the candle of imani.

Each day, make sure to discuss appropriate principle specifically. For the principle of the second day, kujichagulia (self-determination), Jessica Harris, the author of several books on African cooking, mentions Cinque, of the slave ship Amistad, as one who fought for freedom. This can open up a discussion of slavery. On the fourth day, think hard about ujamaa (cooperative economics) and how it can transform communities. On the sixth day, kuumba (creativity), family and friends can make music, passing out instruments and celebrating the creative spirit in all of us, from singers to construction workers. On the last day, imani (faith), you may end with saying, "We have faith in the future and that this year will be a good one for our people and for all the world as we work to strengthen our communities and to achieve peace in the world."

Some of the food prepared for traditional Kwanzaa celebrations are sweet potato pie, fried chicken, red beans and rice, steamed kale, and honey-glazed potatoes. Gifts, the zawadi, are not to be expensive but to be thoughtfully chosen to help children more fully understand the principles of Kwanzaa and their heritage.